Differential Cogitation

An SOP for problem-solving and creative thinking

Bryan Law LL.D.

For illustrating purposes, some of the cases quoted in this book have been modified to hide the entities involved.

First Edition – August 2020

© Fox College of Business

Differential Cogitation

www.differentialcogitation.com

Table of Contents

Introduction

Problem-solving is a crucial technique every individual, corporation, organization and government needs. It requires different thinking methods to generate ideas to solve problems effectively.

People always say, *"Think outside of the box!"* and show you success stories of such a creative method, but no one can show you exactly ***How to think outside the box?***

Learning how to think creatively is like learning how to drive a car. The engineers may tell you how a car works, the mechanism of an engine, the transmission, steering and braking systems. They may also tell you all the terminologies of a vehicle, brake bias, fuel injection, PSI, etc. However, knowing all those things will not make you a good driver. People who ask you to *"Think outside of the box!"* are like shouting *"Drive Safe!"* to a teenager without a driver's license but who tries to drive a car. They cannot help or teach the teenager how to drive just by asking them to do so. A book that tells you how your brain works or how to define problem-solving techniques cannot help or teach you how to think creatively. In other words, you cannot think outside the box just by knowing the terminologies and how our brain works.

Many scholars in neuroscience and psychology have talked about how our brain works or how it affects our behaviour. However, those studies have nothing to do with creativity training. The relationship is like the

1

one between medical doctors and athletic training. You will not consult a doctor about playing basketball or football well, although sports are related to our body. Similarly, we will not consult a neurologist or a psychologist about thinking more creatively, although it relates to our brain.

Having that said, it is still necessary to talk about some terminologies and theories in the thinking process, especially in this introduction section. You should know why people always ask you to *Think outside of the box!*" even the "outside the box" ideas may not apply to your situation. You should also know how we can use different thinking modes in selecting the best idea from all possible solutions.

The most basic and standard thinking modes people use are Convergent Thinking and Divergent Thinking.

Convergent Thinking, also called vertical thinking, is a term coined by Joy Paul Guilford[1]. By its name, it converges or combines different ideas to meet at a point to solve a problem; thus, it generally means the process of finding a single, well-established and best solution to a problem. It is associated with evaluation, analysis, judgment, and decision-making, and it brings together information focused on solving the problem. It is a process of taking many ideas, sorting and evaluating them, and analyzing the pros and cons to make a decision.

Convergent thinking puts the focus on the problem and is a linear and systematic method to arrive at a solution. It narrows down multiple ideas to get one

---

[1]   "Convergent thinking", Wikipedia, last accessed August 28, 2020,
    https://en.wikipedia.org/wiki/Convergent_thinking

single solution and highly involves analytical work. In the convergent thinking mode, people often have to ask, "What is the best solution?" and "Why do we do this?" This method contrasts Divergent Thinking[2], also coined by Joy Paul Guilford.

Divergent thinking, also known as horizontal thinking, works differently from convergent thinking. By its name, it diverges or separates a problem in different directions. Instead of finding a single, well-established, best solution, divergent thinking is the process of coming up with several ideas and possibilities, often without judgment and analysis, to solve a problem. Such ideas may or may not be solutions to the problem; some may even not be feasible because judgment is deferred to accept as many potential solutions as possible.

Divergent thinking encourages different opinions to explore multiple creative ideas. It is a flexible, open-ended and iterative process for solution-finding. Since it looks for multiple possible solutions, it is a 'horizontal' thinking mode compared to the vertical convergent thinking mode, which looks for a single answer. In divergent thinking mode, people often have to ask, "What are the possible solutions?" and "Why don't we do this?". This line of questioning differs from that in convergent thinking, which involves asking, "What is the best solution?" and "Why do we do this?"

Divergent thinking is often used in conjunction with convergent thinking. First, we come up with different ideas by divergent thinking and then use convergent thinking to arrive at one solution, which

[2]   "Divergent thinking", Wikipedia, last accessed August 28, 2020, https://en.wikipedia.org/wiki/Divergent_thinking

should be the 'best' solution. Say we can use divergent thinking mode to create 100 ideas, and we use convergent thinking mode to pick 1 out of 10 ideas. Eventually, we had ten screened ideas after the first round and a single idea after the second round.

The process typically starts with using the Brainstorming[3] and Nominal Group Technique[4] to generate ideas, using an Affinity Diagram[5] to organize the ideas, using Cumulative Voting[6] to screen the ideas, rank them, and discussing the pros and cons of the ideas, including their restraints, costs and feasibilities. The best solution is then selected.

There are other sub-divided or varied thinking modes, such as creative thinking, critical thinking, lateral thinking and parallel thinking. They explain or promote the process by which ideas can be generated and selected. All these thinking modes can be compared to production lines of ideas – we input ideas, modify them, evaluate them, rate them and pick the final solution from the set of ideas. However, none of them reveals precisely how you can create ideas. The biggest challenge in problem-solving is, in fact, "How do you come up with an idea?"

One of my friends worked for a consumer product company, and one of their products had over 90% of the market share. One day, their vice president asked all the managers to explore different ways to increase the consumption of their products. They tried the

---

[3]   "Brainstorming", Wikipedia, last accessed August 28, 2020,
      https://en.wikipedia.org/wiki/Brainstorming
[4]   "Nominal group technique", Wikipedia, last accessed August 28, 2020,
      https://en.wikipedia.org/wiki/Nominal_group_technique
[5]   "Affinity diagram", Wikipedia, last accessed August 28, 2020,
      https://en.wikipedia.org/wiki/Affinity_diagram
[6]   "Cumulative voting", Wikipedia, last accessed August 28, 2020,
      https://en.wikipedia.org/wiki/Cumulative_voting

Brainstorming technique, but no manager could generate any idea or suggestion. Moreover, all the methods mentioned above have the same limitation – they do not provide thorough guidance to solve a problem step by step. That is, one cannot guarantee that a problem can be solved by applying those thinking modes.

Learning how to think creatively is also like learning how to swim. We know our body density is slightly less than that of water. We will float on the water slightly because our body is lighter than water. When we are nervous, our muscles will contract, and our density will be slightly higher than water, so we will sink. However, knowing these will not make you know how to swim. We need a systematic method to learn how to swim.

Over 99% of new inventions and ideas are based on existing facts or concepts. It is extremely difficult, if not impossible, to create an idea that is 100% independent of all existing ideas.

For example, the first wheel is believed to be made of wood[7]. Ancient people may have seen big broken trunks rolled from the hills, and they trimmed the trunks to make wheels. From there, all the ideas and inventions related to cars, gears, disks, and similar products were based on the concept of the wheel.

On the other hand, the people in the Stone Age could not possibly fathom how a computer would be useful, let alone how to produce one. Most, if not all, inventions are based on the knowledge and facts known to the inventors. If there were no birds and insects in

---

[7] "Wheel", Wikipedia, last accessed August 28, 2020, https://en.wikipedia.org/wiki/Wheel

the world, people might never have thought of flying, and the airplane may have never been invented.

Differential cogitation is a problem-solving thinking system that provides an effective way of finding solutions and, more importantly, systematic ways of generating ideas by knowing the different ways of improving existing ideas and concepts. With Differential Cogitation, we can solve a problem effectively and efficiently by systematically generating creative ideas from all existing ideas, even if they are unrelated to our work field.

In Differential Cogitation, *Creative thinking* involves seven techniques that can efficiently solve problems with fresh ideas and alternatives and apply different ideas to different tasks. They are as follows:

Colouring

Removal

Enlargement

Reduction

Transposition

Mapping

Dimension

We will have their full explanations in the coming chapters.

Chapter 1: Colouring

All corporations require new ideas for their products, services and promotions. Honestly, most of the "inventions" are just modifications of the old ones. At first, people invented wheels, and then they invented carts and carriages based on the wheels. Bicycles were invented by improving the carts, and then the motorcar was invented by adding an engine to it. We could say that the airplane was invented by adding wings to the car and converting the engine from powering the wheels to powering the propeller. In other words, modifying an old invention may create a new one and modifying an old idea may also create a new one. Sometimes, we can even reuse an old idea, which may give us a new effect. All the tools in the following chapters are techniques for modifying, reusing, or copying an existing idea to make it a new one.

Colouring in Differential Cogitation means adding something to an existing idea to become a new idea. Although this concept is not new, many people do not know how to apply it or are not able to maximize its power. This concept is similar to value-added products, which is why many products tell you that they are a "Plus". The name such as "XX Plus" is a self-explanatory example of this concept.

Highlighting hair is a simple example to illustrate how Colouring can improve existing things. Although just a few hairs are coloured, the effect is outstanding. The following examples may give you more insights on how to use the Colouring technique to get creative ideas.

Pens

The quill pen was the first type of pen that used ink to write. It is made from the feathers of a large bird, such as a goose, swan, or turkey. Since the tip (the slit) needs sharpening on and off until there is little left of it and it cannot be used. Therefore, people improved it by adding a metal nib to it. Later, it became a nib pen with a wood or metal holder instead of a feather.

A fountain pen was invented by adding a reservoir of ink to a nib pen. People do not have to dip ink to write anymore. Caps were also added to fountain pens to prevent the ink from spilling or running out from the nib. However, in order to be more effective in preventing the ink from leaking or spilling, a metal ball was added to the nib, and ball pens were created.

All the pens we described so far cannot be used upside down as the ink needs gravity to come out of the tube. Knowing that reason, a manufacturer added compressed air to an enclosed ink tube to produce a pen that people could write upside down. The ink of such a pen is forced out by the compressed air when the ball is rolling instead of using gravity so that the nib of the pen does not have to point downward to write.

How do people further improve ball pens nowadays? I would say they are still using the same basic technique – Colouring. Some manufacturers simply add gold and diamonds to the body of their pens to make them pieces of jewelry instead of writing instruments. I have seen some people keep their luxury pens in their shirt pockets to show off but will never use them. With this type of addition, manufacturers can produce unlimited new styles of pens using different designs, just like the jewelry itself.

Cell Phone Manufacturers

In the quest to make the best cell phone, cell phone manufacturers tried to add more features to their cell phones in addition to making the connections faster and more secure.

The first-generation cell phones were based on analog technology and were only used for voice communication. That is, they could only make and receive phone calls (we will talk about how people would have the concept of a cell phone in the next chapter). Once the first cell phone was made, the next step was to improve it. The second-generation cell phones became digital, and text messaging functions were added to them along with simple games. Some small companies were capable of making a good amount of profit by providing games to the cell phone manufacturers by charging a license fee of only one cent per phone.

In the third generation, email, web browsing, video and picture-sharing functions were introduced. After that, all cell phones are produced with a built-in camera. I remember, at the time, my cell phone had a camera added to the flipped body, although we were using the 2G network that did not support the multimedia sharing function. Still, I loved that cell phone as the built-in camera provided convenience to the users, such as when there was a car accident and photos needed to be taken.

The fourth-generation cell phones are almost like mini-computers. Multimedia and internet functions are added to the phones. With the capability of running apps, many features are added to cell phones, such as GPS, OCR, voice typing, image editing and more. By adding new features to smartphones, manufacturers are able to sell over one billion new cell phones worldwide each year.

More features are added to the new cell phones, such as cameras with three or more sensors to capture pictures under extreme low-light environments and provide better stability. They become fully waterproof or even water-resistant to protect the phone from rain or dropping into the water. They provide better security and privacy protection for payment methods and internet browsing. They also come with more rigid screens and bodies so that no protective cases or screen protectors are needed anymore.

Detergent Manufacturers

There are different types of detergents, and the two main types in the consumer product market are laundry detergent and dish detergent.

When the manufacturers of laundry detergents wanted to improve their products, most of them used the technique of Colouring. Some of them added scents to the detergents to give them a fresh feeling after washing. Some of them added bleaching agents to the detergents for a better cleaning effect; while some of the bleaching agents are chlorine-based, most of them are peroxide-based.

Many people have to use drying machines to dry their clothes, especially in the wintertime. Static and wrinkles are the problems associated with drying machines. Therefore, people have to use dryer sheets that contain fabric softener to eliminate them, which also makes clothes feel softer and smell better. Later, fabric softener was added to laundry detergents to serve the same purposes, which created a great new product.

Similarly, scents were added to dish detergents to give different types of smells. Antibiotic chemicals are also added to the dish detergents to kill bacteria such as E. coli, salmonella and staph on dishes. There are two types of dish detergents: one is for dishwashers, and the other is for hand washing.

For the hand wash type, many manufacturers added the hand soap function so that people can use the detergents for both dishes and hands. However, dish detergents are designed to deal mainly with grease, so they are more likely to strip our hands of the natural oils, leaving them feeling dry and stiff. Therefore, some manufacturers added moisturizing agents to them to prevent dry hands. Many of them also added biodegradable functions to the detergents to make them more environmentally friendly. For industrial-use hand soaps, the manufacturers add pumice to the soaps to rub the tough grease. All these new types of detergents are 'invented' by the Colouring technique.

Shampoo Manufacturers

Since we have the 2-in-1 shampoo (shampoo plus conditioner), many shampoo manufacturers have also added another function to their shampoos – shower gel. Most of these 3-in-1 shampoos are advertised as a Sport Shampoo or an After Sport Shampoo with the body wash function.

With the 2-in-1 and 3-in-1 concepts, shampoo manufacturers may have N-in-1 ideas to make new types of shampoos. For example, a bubble bath function can be added to the shower gel function for those people who want to take a bubble bath instead of a shower.

Most of the manufacturers had already added fragrance to shampoos. Once they add a suitable scent to it, they can call it a 4-in-1 shampoo with cologne or perfume use. Similarly, if the deodorant is added to the shampoo, it will become a 5-in-1 shampoo. If the antiperspirant is added, it will become a 6-in-1 shampoo.

Toothpaste

Actually, toothpaste has been modified by the Colouring technique well ahead of detergents and shampoos for years. Originally, modern toothpaste was used only for cleaning purposes. Later, ingredients such as menthol were added to it to give users a refreshing feeling and neutralize bad breath odours. Fluoride was added to toothpaste as an effective anticavity dentifrice[8].

Different types of chemicals are added to toothpaste to provide various types of functions. They can prevent plaque buildup, whiten teeth, strengthen enamel, ease sensitive teeth, reduce gum bleeding and gum inflammation, or kill bacteria on teeth, the tongue, cheeks and gums.

Cigarettes

A tobacco manufacturer wanted to produce a new brand of cigarettes, but they had already produced different brands of cigarettes by using different types of tobacco. *How do you make a fresh taste of cigarettes?* They changed the question to *What should be added to the cigarettes to create a fresh taste?* The answer was, of course, chemicals such as menthol and other fruit favouring compounds.

Adding other substances to tobacco to make cigarettes is not a secret in the industry. A typical chemical added is ammonia, as it can make the nicotine easier to be absorbed into our body, hence can make the

---

8   "Toothpaste", Wikipedia, last accessed August 28, 2020,
     https://en.wikipedia.org/wiki/Toothpaste

cigarette more addictive[9]. Nicotine is also added to some tobacco products such as e-cigarettes, and they can control the e-cigarettes to contain nicotine at different levels.

To provide a "healthier" product, tobacco companies added filters to the cigarette to reduce the intake of harmful chemicals such as tar and nicotine. However, filtered cigarettes are not necessarily healthier than unfiltered ones because a seasoned smoker needs his daily dose of nicotine, although the intake of nicotine per cigarette is reduced. *Therefore, the person will feel the urge to smoke until he gets his full dose for that particular period. Essentially, he will end up smoking more cigarettes to get the same fix[10].*

Tracked Vehicles

After automobiles are invented, people always face the problems of driving them on muddy roads or sandy roads as the vehicles will lose their traction and may lose control. It is also a challenge to drive them on the beach or in deep snow.

If a vehicle is stuck on a beach or in deep snow, experienced drivers know that they have to reduce the tire pressure (to deflate the tires) to provide more traction between the tires and the ground so that they can safely maneuver across the sand or snow. Actually, the real trick is to increase the contact area between the tires and the ground so that the traction can also be increased.

---

[9] "Chemicals in Every Cigarette", The United States Food and Drug Administration, last updated December 19, 2017, https://www.fda.gov/tobacco-products/products-ingredients-components/chemicals-every-cigarette

[10] "Are Filtered Cigarettes Safer Than Unfiltered Ones?", Science ABC, last updated October 19, 2019, https://www.scienceabc.com/humans/reason-manufacturers-hide-things-filtered-cigarettes.html

However, it does not matter how big the wheels are; the contact surface between a wheel and the ground is only a small area (a single point if we view the vehicle from the side). That is why we have to deflate the tires to make the contact surface bigger to drive a car on a beach or snow. From the concept of connecting two gears (like the mechanism of a bicycle), people found out that they could increase the contact surface by adding a belt to connect the wheels. Therefore, a continuous track is added to the wheels to provide more traction, and continuous tracks are added to agricultural tractors, all-terrain vehicles and all other off-road vehicles. Military vehicles such as tanks also use tracks to make them all-terrain vehicles.

Fax Machine

Many people say a fax machine is a combination of a telephone and a photocopier. That is only true to explain the concept of it but not for the invention. In fact, the first fax machine[11] was invented and patented in 1846, but the first telephone[12] was invented later and patented in 1876. The first photocopier[13] was invented in 1887, and the first commercial photocopier was patented in 1959.

Practically, a fax machine may be the concept of adding graphics to telegraphy[14]. Nonetheless, it is a product that adds the features of telecommunication and photographic reproduction. Later, the feature of transmitting and reproducing colour copies was also added to fax machines.

---

[11] "Fax", Wikipedia, last accessed August 28, 2020, https://en.wikipedia.org/wiki/Fax
[12] "Telephone", Wikipedia, last accessed August 28, 2020, https://en.wikipedia.org/wiki/Telephone
[13] "Photocopier", Wikipedia, last accessed August 28, 2020, https://en.wikipedia.org/wiki/Photocopier
[14] "Telegraphy", Wikipedia, last accessed August 28, 2020, https://en.wikipedia.org/wiki/Telegraphy

Watch

The first-generation watches had very low accuracy and might have an error several hours per day[15] until the minute hand was added to the face. Yes, the original design had only the hour hand. Later on, the second hand was also added to some watches to show their excellence in accuracy.

Later, the functions to display the day of the week, the date, and the month of the year were also added to some watches, which are not easy jobs for mechanical watches. Some watch manufacturers also added a function to show the phase of the moon in order to tell if it is the morning or afternoon. Some watches have more than one dial to tell the times in different time zones.

Electronic watches have added more functions, such as alarm clocks, altimeters, barometers, calendars, calorie counters, compasses, emails, GPS, heart rate monitors, stopwatches, survival emergency calls and tachymeters. Cell phone features, including Bluetooth and Wi-fi functions, have also been added to some watches.

Eyeglasses

So far, it seems that the Colouring technique is simple, but sometimes it might take people hundreds of years to make a simple improvement by applying it. Maybe it is because the people at that time did not know how to apply the Colouring technique systematically yet.

---

[15] "Watch", Wikipedia, last accessed August 28, 2020, https://en.wikipedia.org/wiki/Watch

For example, eyeglasses were invented in the late thirteenth century[16] , but it took more than 400 years to invent the sunglasses[17]. Although sunglasses were just to add colour to the lenses of eyeglasses and stained glass was founded in churches and monasteries since the seventh century, people did not use stained glass to make sunglasses until one thousand years later.

Since sunglasses are mainly used in outdoor activities, it makes sense to add a band to the temples (arms) to secure the glasses during the activities. Such bands are also good for ordinary eyeglasses for indoor sports such as basketball and badminton.

Consequently, goggles were made to cover the driver's and pilot's eyes better[18]. It was done by adding fabrics and expanding the eyeglasses glasses to cover the face better. Such a creative technique can be the Colouring, or the Enlargement technique talked about in Chapter 3.

Seaplane

At the beginning of this chapter, we talked about the inventions of carts, carriages, bicycles, motorcars and finally, the airplane. The invention of the seaplane[19] took fewer stages, and, interestingly, it was invented more or less at the same time as the invention of the airplane[20].

---

[16]   "Glasses", Wikipedia, last accessed August 28, 2020,
       https://en.wikipedia.org/wiki/Glasses
[17]   "Sunglasses", Wikipedia, last accessed August 28, 2020,
       https://en.wikipedia.org/wiki/Sunglasses
[18]   "Goggles", Wikipedia, last accessed August 28, 2020,
       https://en.wikipedia.org/wiki/Goggles
[19]   "Seaplane", Wikipedia, last accessed August 28, 2020,
       https://en.wikipedia.org/wiki/Seaplane
[20]   "Airplane", Wikipedia, last accessed August 28, 2020,
       https://en.wikipedia.org/wiki/Airplane

Again, the invention of the seaplane was done by Colouring. People added wings and engines to a boat hull to make a seaplane.

Poutine

Compared to other popular cuisines, poutine is a relatively new dish. Although it is getting more and more attention from the public, many people still do not know what exactly poutine is and where it originated.

Poutine is a dish that includes french fries and cheese curds topped with brown gravy. It originated in the Canadian province of Quebec and emerged in the late 1950s in the Centre-du-Québec area[21].

Simply speaking, poutine is a new dish that adds cheese and gravy to french fries.

---

[21] "Poutine", Wikipedia, last accessed August 28, 2020, https://en.wikipedia.org/wiki/Poutine

Chapter 2: Removal

New ideas can be created by removing or reducing some unnecessary or unwanted components of old ideas, known as Removal. When people are used to seeing colour images, a black-and-white image may attract attention. That is a simple example to illustrate how Removal can improve existing functionality. The following examples may give you more insights into using the Removal technique to get creative ideas; some used both Colouring and Removal techniques to improve the old ideas.

Telephone

A single-unit telephone is the simplest case to be handled by telecommunication companies. A private branch exchange system[22] will be needed when a building or organization has many users and wants to share the telephone lines.

Actually, the first-generation telephones had no dials, and the users needed to tell the operator which terminal they wanted to connect to. Later, the need for operators was removed using a key telephone system for single-line users. However, operators were still required for the private branch exchange until the systems were totally automatic.

The telephone set had to be improved too. People felt that it was inconvenient to use a phone as the user

---

[22] "Business telephone system", Wikipedia, last accessed August 28, 2020, https://en.wikipedia.org/wiki/Business_telephone_system

had to stay at the location where the telephone was located. That was because the telephone handset had to connect with the main unit with a cord. If we remove the cord, the user could be more mobile. That was the logic of making cordless phones.

Both cordless phones and cell phones had antennas attached to them when they were invented. The antennas made the cell phones too bulky to be carried or pocketed, especially for female cell phone users. Nowadays, the designs of all cordless phones and cell phone bodies have been streamlined without an antenna. The only exception may be satellite phones, which use big antennas to increase their transmission power.

Some cell phone companies have removed the headphone jack to increase water resistance. Similarly, some manufacturers may remove the power switch and the charging port to maximize the water-resistant feature.

Optical Eyeglasses

The lenses for optical eyeglasses were all made from glasses in the past; that is why they are called glasses. Most of the frames at that time were made from metal, mainly steel alloy. Both the weights of the glasses and frame were heavy. Often, you would find two dark marks on your nose even after wearing the glasses for just a while. The main problem to be solved was *How to reduce the weight of eyeglasses?*

The first thing people did was to replace metal frames with plastic ones. Half-rimless frames were created since the plastic frames can clip the lenses more securely. Such a design could reduce almost half the weight of the frames pressed on our noses. With the improvement in technology, plastic lenses were also used, significantly reducing the weight of eyeglasses.

Once plastic lenses were available, people started using rimless frames, which further reduced the total weight. Polycarbonate lenses make eyewear more durable and also lighter than plastic lenses.

Contact lenses were invented to totally eliminate the weight of eyeglass frames and significantly reduce the weight of the lenses. After reducing the size to produce contact lenses by using the Removal technique, colourful contact lenses are produced by applying the Colouring technique.

Undergarments

The first type of undergarments for ladies in the fourth century was breast-bands[23]. Fragments of linen textiles found in Austria in the fifteenth century are believed to have been bras with two shoulder straps. More supportive materials were added to the bras to hold and train the torso into a desired shape, and that is how the corset was created.

Although straps were added to the undergarments to fix their position and hard materials were used in the corset to support the body shape, the straps were removed to produce another type of undergarments so that the undergarments could be well covered, softer and more comfortable.

The idea of modern breast-bands, known as bra tubes, was to remove unnecessary parts of a T-shirt such that the remaining part can cover the breast. On the other hand, elastic materials are added to make sure that they can hold themselves in the desired position without using straps.

---

[23] "Bra", Wikipedia, last accessed August 28, 2020, https://en.wikipedia.org/wiki/Bra

Underpants manufacturers have also reduced the size material of men's and women's panties by using different shapes, from long underwear to boxers, from boxers to bikinis and from bikinis to G-strings, to provide newer styles of undergarments.

Water

Many soft drinks are made by adding sugar, carbon dioxide gas, colourings and other chemicals to the water. The manufacturers may simply add minerals to water to make mineral water and add carbon dioxide to it to make carbonated water. On the other hand, some people just like water and prefer distilled or filtered water. Therefore, the manufacturers have to remove or reduce the impurities in the water.

For water treatment, we can use Colouring or Removal to deal with it. With the Colouring technique, chlorine gas is added to the water to kill the germs and bacteria. However, chlorine itself is a contaminant, and when chlorine mixes with organic matter, it forms new chemicals that remain in the water and are classified as possible causes of cancer, specifically bladder cancer[24]. As a result, many public facilities such as libraries and community centres have water filters installed in their drinking water fountains to *remove* the chlorine chemicals.

I bought a reverse osmosis[25] system from a popular water purification system company a few years ago. When I bought the replacement filter at their shop one day, the owner introduced a 'miracle system' to me

---

[24] "Chlorination by-products", Canadian Cancer Society, last accessed August 28, 2020, https://www.cancer.ca/en/prevention-and-screening/ reduce-cancer-risk/make-informed-decisions/know-your-environment/chlorination-by-products/

[25] "Reverse osmosis", Wikipedia, last accessed August 28, 2020, https://en.wikipedia.org/wiki/Reverse_osmosis

– an amethyst crystal-infused water unit to be installed at the water faucet in the kitchen. He said the amethyst would dissolve into the water on a microscale, and the water infused with the natural soothing crystal could promote calm and peace. It could relieve headaches, tension, and physical and psychological stress.

Such a type of game to add and remove particles in the water will never end.

Light Bulbs

The old incandescent light bulbs are electric lights with a tungsten filament heated until it glows. Often, the filament melted when it became too hot, and the bulb had to be replaced.

By the conservation of energy, if the light bulbs are heated, that means some of the electric energy is not used to transform to light energy but to heat energy instead. In other words, tungsten-filament light bulbs are not energy-efficient. Making it more energy-efficient became the goal to reduce the heat generated. When the heat generated is reduced (by using another technology), the life span of light bulbs is also increased. That is, manufacturers improved the light bulbs by reducing the energy loss to heat and increasing their life span.

Although LED light bulbs have significantly reduced energy consumption, the power of this type of light bulb is not comparable to other types, such as halogen lamps[26] and compact fluorescent lamps[27]. That is, we have to add power to the newer light bulbs,

---

[26] "Halogen lamp", Wikipedia, last accessed August 28, 2020, https://en.wikipedia.org/wiki/Halogen_lamp

[27] "Compact fluorescent lamp", Wikipedia, last accessed August 28, 2020, https://en.wikipedia.org/wiki/Compact_fluorescent_lamp

although we have successfully reduced their energy consumption. After using the Removal technique, we have to use the Enlargement technique to improve it further. The "Enlargement" technique will be discussed in the next chapter.

Frames

We are not sure if it was the result of mathematicians' suggestions or based on trial and error, but carpenters know that a rectangular frame or a square frame is not stable and will easily change its shape to a parallelogram. The same problem happens to all quadrilaterals, and it will be worse if we change the frame to a pentagon. The more side we add to the frame, the more unstable the frame will be. However, a rectangular frame will become stable when we reduce it from four sides to three sides. Changing the quadrilateral frame to a triangular one will make it more durable.

Similarly, we found that a table may not be stable when the floor is not flat. This problem can be solved by reducing the legs of the table to three only. It is because we are in a 3-dimensional world. The first leg fixes the location of the X-axis (the latitude), the second leg fixes the location of the Y-axis (the longitude), and the third leg fixes the location of the Z-axis (the altitude).

The same principle applies to a tripod. However, when people wanted a lighter and smaller "tripod", they reduced the number of legs of a tripod from three to one, and the new product is called a monopod[28].

Cigarettes

---

[28] "Monopod", Wikipedia, last accessed August 28, 2020, https://en.wikipedia.org/wiki/Monopod

24

In the previous chapter, we talked about tobacco companies adding nicotine to their product to make people more addicted to their products. Many of them did it by genetically engineering their tobacco crops to contain two times the amount of nicotine[29]. On the other hand, they provide 'healthier' cigarettes by reducing or removing some of the ingredients in their tobacco products. Light cigarettes are produced by lowering the tar levels.

Although many people think light cigarettes are better for their health (or not as bad as the regular ones), *light* cigarettes *have been shown to be no safer than regular cigarettes, and smoking them does not lower the risk of cancer or other diseases*[30]. Reducing harmful substances in tobacco products may just be a gimmick, but it increases sales.

Metal Sculptures

In ancient times, metal statues were small in size as metals were rare and expensive. In some countries, trading metals without the government's approval was even illegal. Therefore, most colossal statues were non-metal and were carved into the surface of caves or rocks of mountains. A more recent and popular one is Mount Rushmore.

When colossal metal statues are made, all of them are hollow as it is not only expensive to cast solid metal statues but also too heavy to hold them above ground and transport a solid one. The Removal method

---

[29] "How Big Tobacco made cigarettes more addictive", Truth Initiative, last updated January 23, 2018, https://truthinitiative.org/research-resources/harmful-effects-tobacco/how-big-tobacco-made-cigarettes-more-addictive

[30] "light cigarette", National Cancer Institute, last accessed August 28, 2020, https://www.cancer.gov/publications/dictionaries/cancer-terms/def/light-cigarette

is now applied to jewelry and decor made with precious metals.

I have seen a 24K gold Buddha statue the size of a large suitcase. If it was a solid gold statue, its weight would have been over 1,000 kg and would be worth more than fifty million dollars. However, it was a hollow one with the latest technology to make the gold as thin as possible. The weight was less than two kilograms, so the price was only about one hundred thousand dollars. Since it is not gold plated, it is advertised as 24K gold or pure gold. However, it is very fragile, so it must be put into a clear box for display.

Fashion Design

Fashion design is one of the industries that always needs new ideas. That is one of the areas in which all of the creative thinking techniques in this book can be applied. We can always use the Colouring technique to add something new to a fashion style to give it a new look. For example, adding a tie or bowtie to a lady's gown, adding a pocket square to a jean jacket, or adding crystal grains on the service of running shoes are some designers' styles that applied the Colouring technique. We will talk about the use of the Dimension technique in fashion design in Chapter 7.

To use the technique of Removal, we have to think about the picture of a full set of garments first; then, we will start removing items from it. A typical man's suit comprises a shirt, a tie, a suit jacket, trousers, socks and dress shoes. We may take out the tie or the jacket to make it less formal. Although there is no unique definition of the term 'business casual', it was developed by removing something like the tie and jacket from a formal dress to make it casual.

Fashion designers use the Removal technique to modify casual dressings more often. In their fashion shows, they would ask their models to wear shoes without wearing socks or wear a tie without wearing a shirt but a T-shirt instead. They would also ask their models to wear a coat or jacket without wearing anything under it, not even the undergarment. After those shows, fashion would follow these styles for years. The Removal technique can be applied to a part instead of the whole piece. For example, we can cut some fabric from the jeans to make the ripped jeans.

Snacks

People always look for 'healthier' foods, including junk foods. Therefore, many manufacturers provide 'healthier' products by lowering the salt, sugar, or fat levels in their products. As a result, we have products like light potato chips, diet pops and skimmed milk ice cream. Gluten-free and transfat-free foods are now very common. Of course, we have decaffeinated coffee, tea and cola too.

What else can people reduce or remove from their food products?

Carbs and milk!

Restaurants now provide keto pizzas that are low in carbohydrates. Some even provide keto vegan pizzas with dairy-free cheese.

Cleaned Foods

In some supermarkets, it does not matter whether fishes are live or frozen; they are sold without cutting and cleaning. If you want the fish to be cleaned and cut, you have to pay a higher price (say, $0.30 more per pound). Traditionally, fish are sold as fillets that are descaled, cut, deboned, cleaned and packed. The prices are much higher than the fish sold as whole pieces, fresh or frozen.

A well-established trading company was founded by the owner, who initially sold only cleaned dried beans and rice in the local market decades ago. At that time, dried beans and rice were always mixed with dirt, sand and even stone chips. The owner provided labour to screen out the unwanted materials from those foods and sold them at higher but affordable prices. Once he got enough capital, the owner put peeled garlic in small bottles and soaked them in oil. The extra costs were minimal, but they were sold at a premium price. Such a huge success enabled the owner to found an international food trading company.

Alcoholic Beverages

Many people enjoy drinking alcoholic beverages. Some of us like low alcohol content beverages such as cider and wine coolers, some like medium alcohol content beverages such as wines and fortified wines, and some like high alcohol content beverages such as vodka, whisky and brandy. The alcohol content in some spirits can be higher than 95%.

On the other hand, some people like to have the taste of alcoholized beverages but may not want to consume alcohol or cannot consume it because of health reasons such as pregnancy. Therefore, some companies provide dealcoholized beverages such as dealcoholized wine and beer.

Sometimes, it may not be a supply-demand reason to reduce or remove the alcohol content in the beverages, but because of the laws. In some jurisdictions, stores and supermarkets are only allowed to sell beverages less than a certain alcohol level, say 1%. The companies will, therefore, produce some beverages with alcohol levels lower than that legal limit so that these kinds of products can be sold in stores and supermarkets to increase their sales.

Healthier Foods

To some consumers, food that is not white is not a good thing; even the colour is a natural one that appears in foods. Therefore, people provide white flour by bleaching it, white sugar by refining it and white rice by stripping its bran and germ. These white products had better market shares until people started considering their downsides. Consequently, many of these products are left in their raw state to provide healthier foods to consumers, especially those who are sensitive to chemical intake. In fact, many manufacturers always play with such addition and removal tricks.

Trolleybus

Many cities have trams as their public transit[31], which normally use the track as the return path for their electricity supply[32]. The track is run over by other vehicles on the road, thus needs higher maintenance costs. As a result, the idea of a trackless tram was generated, and the trolleybus[33] was created.

Trolleybuses still draw electrical power from the overhead wires, but they use the wires as the return path instead of the track. Therefore, the track can be removed. However, trolleybuses still have limitations and maintenance issues with the overhead wires. In order to remove the overhead wires, batteries are added to the buses as the power supply.

Paperless Books

---

[31] "Trolleybus usage by country", Wikipedia, last accessed August 28, 2020, https://en.wikipedia.org/wiki/Trolleybus_usage_by_country

[32] "Tram", Wikipedia, last accessed August 28, 2020, https://en.wikipedia.org/wiki/Tram

[33] "Trolleybus", Wikipedia, last accessed August 28, 2020, https://en.wikipedia.org/wiki/Trolleybus

One hundred years ago, people could never imagine how to make a book without using paper or other tangible materials. Now, computer technology makes paperless books possible. Even if the books have colourful diagrams, we can make the eBooks[34] the same readability as the paper version.

Actually, paperless books had been made at least fifty years ago. My first paperless book was a storybook in tape produced in 1972. We did not have to read the book; we could play it on a cassette tape player, and the stories would be told. Later, storybooks were stored in CD, VCD and DVD formats before the eBooks were created.

---

[34] "E-book", Wikipedia, last accessed August 28, 2020, https://en.wikipedia.org/wiki/E-book

Chapter 3: Enlargement

The Chinese invented gunpowder[35], which was one of the four great inventions[36]. However, the original use of gunpowder was only for entertainment and celebrations, such as making firecrackers and fireworks. Later, it was applied to military use by increasing the quantity of gunpowder to make bombs, which were like huge firecrackers. The fire lance[37] was invented by tying a big firecracker to a spear that would explode to hurt people when it reached the enemy.

In the military, increasing the amount of dynamite in a bomb (in multiples) will definitely increase the lethality of that bomb. That is the basic concept of the Enlargement technique, which normally means multiplying or magnifying.

Enlargement can be focused just on a particular part or function, on the whole item or concept. The following examples may give you some insights on how to use the technique of Enlargement to get creative ideas; some of them used other techniques in addition to Enlargement to improve the old ideas.

Mass Production

---

[35] "Gunpowder", Wikipedia, last accessed August 28, 2020,
https://en.wikipedia.org/wiki/Gunpowder
[36] "Four Great Inventions", Wikipedia, last accessed August 28, 2020,
https://en.wikipedia.org/wiki/Four_Great_Inventions
[37] "Fire lance", Wikipedia, last accessed August 28, 2020,
https://en.wikipedia.org/wiki/Fire_lance

The first example of using the Enlargement technique to solve problems is mass production. When a vase is handmade, it is a piece of art, but the production cost is high due to the person-hours spent on it. The production cost will be reduced when we multiply the production scale by standardizing the size and design and using a production line to make the vases. The cost will be further and significantly reduced once the machinery is introduced.

In general, due to economies of scale, the more products produced, the lower the production cost. Of course, mass production has its pros and cons; overcapacity is one of the disadvantages if the overall production cannot be well estimated and controlled.

World Records

On and off, we would hear the news of catching the biggest shark in the world, hunting the largest moose in the world, and growing the largest tomato in the world. Such kind of news is never-ending. While we may not control how big the wild animals will grow, and there is no guarantee that we can grow a record-breaking melon or tomato, it is always possible to make a big item such as a big pizza, a big table or a big hamburger. When it is big enough to set a new world record, it is the best gimmick to promote your product or services.

Actually, making a big item does not need to be a world record; it can be an icon or landmark as long as it is big enough. For example, the Big Apple[38] in Ontario is a huge apple-shaped building structure, and the

---

[38] "Big Apple (Colborne, Ontario)", Wikipedia, last accessed August 28, 2020, https://en.wikipedia.org/wiki/Big_Apple _(Colborne,_Ontario)

Gibeau Orange Julep[39] is a massive orange-shaped building structure in Quebec; both of them have become roadside attractions in Canada.

A giant sock or huge glove with a company logo and slogan on it will be a good promotional item for any company, which is not difficult to make, and the cost is relatively low compared to other big items.

Setting a world record is a good marketing gimmick for corporations and a huge satisfaction for individuals. Sometimes, setting a world record may be an achievable task for everyone by using this Enlargement technique. You may be one of the world record holders by joining a group event such as the "Largest gathering of people dressed as Superman[40]" or "Largest cup percussion ensemble[41]".

If you can read, sing, or just blow a whistle, you can be one of the participants in the events such as "Largest reading group", "Largest singing group" or "Largest whistleblowing group". All you have to do is to organize such an event. You do not even have to do anything in some events, such as the "Largest human currency symbol[42]"; all you have to do is to go there to participate.

The Coffee Shop

---

[39] "Gibeau Orange Julep", Wikipedia, last accessed August 28, 2020, https://en.wikipedia.org/wiki/Gibeau_Orange_Julep

[40] "Largest gathering of people dressed as Superman", Guinness World Records Limited, last accessed August 28, 2020, https://www.guinnessworldrecords.com/world-records/largest-gathering-of-people-dressed-as-superman

[41] "Largest cup percussion ensemble",Guinness World Records Limited, last accessed August 28, 2020, https://www.guinnessworldrecords.com/world-records/108602-largest-cup-percussion-ensemble

[42] "Largest human currency symbol", Guinness World Records Limited, last accessed August 28, 2020, https://www.guinnessworldrecords.com/world-records/largest-human-currency-symbol

A friend of mine wanted to open a coffee shop, and his goal was to open several coffee shops one by one and eventually turn them into a franchise business. His problem was: *How can he stand out from the market leaders to capture some of their market shares?*

When I tried to help him, the first technique I considered was Colouring. I thought about adding a new product line to his coffee shop, such as noodles. However, I did not have enough confidence as the demographics in the location of his new coffee shop at that time might not fit such an idea.

The second approach I considered was using both Removal and Colouring. First, I would reduce the dining area of his coffee shop and would add a 'partner' to sublet part of the rented area. For example, he could sublet the coffee shop to a small law firm so that he would have some basic customers (the lawyers, paralegals and their clients) every day and could receive some 'subsidies' from the sublet rent. That could reduce the cost, increase revenue and generate more traffic. However, finding a suitable subtenant was not an easy task, and more importantly, it would limit the growth of the coffee shop chain as it would be more and more difficult for his new coffee shops to find subtenants.

After all, I suggested he use the Enlargement technique to increase the sizes of his coffees, muffins and donuts to at least 50% bigger than those in other coffee shops. Customers could pay the market price of a small coffee to get the size of a medium coffee, but we would still call it a small size. Their homemade muffins and donuts could be twice the size of the others. Such big sizes would not only give the patrons the real benefits of getting more coffee and food but also have a big impact as a marketing program to promote the new coffee shop.

He followed my advice, and such a strategy brought huge success to his coffee shop. Consequently, he opened several more shops in three years. What surprised me was that he did not expand his chain further or franchise his operation as planned. He sold all his coffee shops to different buyers after a few years without consulting me again.

Digital Cameras

We said the Enlargement technique is like magnification. When we talk about magnifying, the first thing that appears in many people's minds may be a magnifying glass. In optical equipment, the power to magnify is called the zooming power.

Before single-lens reflex digital cameras and smartphones were popular, people buying digital cameras would aim at point-and-shoot cameras. They are more affordable and compact in size, so they are also called compact digital cameras. There were about 100 brands that produced compact digital cameras at that time[43], and many people would rely on the zooming power to decide which brand or model they would buy. The zooming power, of course, means optical zoom and not digital zoom.

Other than the zooming power, another feature that the consumers would rely on to pick their compact digital camera was its resolution. The resolution was measured in pixels until the first megapixel digital camera was made. Now, all digital cameras use megapixels to measure their resolution.

Therefore, many digital camera manufacturers focused only on improving the zooming power and

---

[43] "List of digital camera brands", Wikipedia, last accessed August 28, 2020, https://en.wikipedia.org/wiki/List_of_digital_camera_brands

resolution of their cameras. When they marketed and promoted these cameras, they almost only highlighted the optical zoom function and resolution because these were the most important indicators of camera performance.

Televisions

Since the first television[44] was invented more than one hundred years ago, people have been trying to produce televisions with bigger and bigger screens. However, when televisions were produced using the cathode-ray tube[45] (CRT) technology, manufacturers could not just enlarge the screen without enlarging the CRT. Since a CRT needs space to project the electron beams on the screen to create images, a longer TV body will be required to produce a bigger screen. Moreover, the screens of CRT TVs are made of glass and are very heavy. Both factors caused a big television to be too large and heavy to be produced.

Before the invention of plasma, LCD and LED televisions, people used projectors to project video on a white screen to get a big picture. An alternative for big-screen television was to split the electronic signals and project different portions of the image to different televisions, then combine them to give a full picture. This type of "Enlargement" was done by "Colouring" – combining the small televisions to provide a big screen.

Boats

---

44   "Television", Wikipedia, last accessed August 28, 2020, https://en.wikipedia.org/wiki/Television

45   "Cathode-ray tube", Wikipedia, last accessed August 28, 2020, https://en.wikipedia.org/wiki/Cathode-ray_tube

It is believed that the first boat was a dugout[46], which was made from a hollowed tree trunk. Since then, bigger and stronger ships were made to carry more cargo or to be tougher on the battlefields. Now, in each category, the biggest ships of its type are all over 200,000 tonnes in gross tonnage[47].

When a ship is enlarged big enough, it may have functions other than just carrying cargo, passengers, soldiers and weapons. Some facilities on the mainland, such as a nuclear plant, can be built on a ship and made mobile. An aircraft carrier is the best example to show how important it is to expand a warship as it has the functions of a military airbase.

Floating nuclear power stations[48] have been made to provide electricity to remote islands or offshore oil and gas field development, including the Arctic. It is basically a ship large enough to put a nuclear power station on it so that it can sail to those areas to power them. On the other hand, this concept also involves the Reduction technique to diminish a nuclear power station so that it fits into a ship. Such a technique will be discussed in the next chapter.

More than forty years ago, there was a Sci-fi Japanese cartoon that talked about aliens and hegemonism. The protagonists all lived on a self-sufficient, mobile artificial island with a military airbase and arsenal. Although the island was so big that it had all the infrastructures of a small city, it was so mobile that it could travel to any ocean to carry out its

---

[46] "Dugout canoe", Wikipedia, last accessed August 28, 2020,
      https://en.wikipedia.org/wiki/Dugout_canoe
[47] "List of longest ships", Wikipedia, last accessed August 28, 2020,
      https://en.wikipedia.org/wiki/List_of_longest_ships
[48] "Russian floating nuclear power station", Wikipedia, last accessed August 28, 2020,
      https://en.wikipedia.org/wiki/Russian_floating_nuclear_power_station

missions. With the advancement of shipbuilding technology, this idea may soon be put into practice. Such a mobile artificial island may be built by combining many floating structures, which is also the concept of the Colouring technique.

Abstract Paintings

The record of the longest legs of a human individual in the world belongs to a woman and is 132 cm long[49]. With her 200 cm body height, the ratio of her legs' length to body height is 0.660, while the average ratio of legs' length to body height is 0.530[50]. In other words, 0.660 is considered an extreme value of the ratio of leg length to body height. How about a ratio of 0.900? For sure, humans cannot have such a proportion, but it appears in abstract paintings.

Some abstract artists like to exaggerate a particular part of the human body, such as the mouth, breasts, cheeks and buttocks, in their paintings or statues. The common effect is like viewing that part with a magnifying glass. Many artists apply this kind of painting technique to other subjects, including buildings and animals, with a particular part being exaggerated or magnified.

Plush Toys

Kids love plush toys, and so do young ladies and women. Many people buy plush toys for their loved ones as a birthday present, Valentine's Day gift or just a surprise. Since most of the plush toys are now trademarked, the production costs will be higher due to

---

[49] "Svetlana Pankratova", Wikipedia, last accessed August 28, 2020, https://en.wikipedia.org/wiki/Svetlana_Pankratova

[50] "Scaling Calculator", Pennsylvania State University, last accessed August 28, 2020, http://tools.openlab.psu.edu/tools/proportionality_constants.htm

the license fees. The selling prices will also be higher, but the margins may be less than the non-trademarked ones. To compete with those trademarked plush toys, some manufacturers use the Enlargement technique to improve their toys and get more buyers.

Teddy bears, pandas, dolphins, dogs, giraffes, and almost any type of animal can be made as huge plush toys. Many of them are also used as cushions or body pillows in addition to just toys. Their prices are normally in proportion to their size. Although they are not popular characters seen on TV or in movies, they are welcomed by plush toy lovers. In fact, many people regret buying a plush toy that is too big to fit in their room or on their bed.

Pressure Washer Spray Guns

People have used water for cleaning for thousands of years. Since the friction of water is comparatively low, it is difficult to use it for cleaning without using tools such as a brush or a piece of cloth. Experience tells us that we cannot just use a bucket of water to splash it on a concrete floor to clean a speck of sticky dirt. However, if we can significantly increase the power of the water touching the ground, the water will be strong enough to clean the dirt by itself. Pressure washer spray guns are therefore made.

Other than water, spray guns can use most kinds of fluids. Since electronic products such as computers cannot be cleaned by water as they will damage the electronics inside, compressed air is used to clean the dust and dirt on electronic equipment.

Chapter 4: Reduction

The technique of Reduction involves breaking down ideas and concepts, dividing or diminishing them. The four creative techniques so far mentioned, Colouring, Removal, Enlargement and Reduction, are often used in a mix. The following examples may give you some insights on how to use the technique of Reduction to get creative ideas; some of them used other techniques in addition to the Reduction technique to improve the old ideas.

Human Resources

When a company expands or contracts, it may have to increase or decrease its workforce. Often, the human resources department may have to use different methods to deal with it. Human resources professionals use four thinking techniques in different situations.

Colouring:

A company may want to hire more employees when they need to expand, but they may also increase the work hours of their employees, such as paying overtime if it is just a temporary increase in workload. They may also increase the number of shifts to maximize the usage of their equipment and facilities without expanding their factory.

Removal:

Laying off employees is not the only option to reduce payroll expenses. We can use the methods from the Colouring technique above to find out the opposite methods for contractions. When we can increase the work hours of employees by paying overtime wages or adding work shifts, we can also reduce the wages or work hours. There are cases in which companies offered a reduction of work hours to every worker so that all of them could keep their jobs with fewer work hours per week until their crisis was gone. If the employees are not paid hourly, we can also reduce their salaries by a certain percentage. During the financial crisis in 2008, many employers and employees agreed to lower their wages for one year or until the economy could be recovered.

Enlargement:

When an employee is capable, we can increase their job responsibility. Although the wage will be increased accordingly, that is not a Colouring technique, as the number of official work hours will not be increased. For example, a worker was initially only responsible for packing goods in a factory. After being promoted, she is responsible for overseeing the entire production line, from product manufacturing to product packaging. Her scope of work has been multiplied, but her working hours are still 9 to 5.

When a branch manager is promoted to a district manager, and then a regional manager and so on, this process is also an Enlargement technique – to magnify the area that the manager will be responsible for managing and supervising.

Reduction:

The promotion of a general worker to a factory manager to supervise more functions is an Enlargement technique. Making employees specialize in fewer functions or a single function is a Reduction technique.

Division of labour and specialization is a common process in factories, but it also applies to all professions. Before the automatic production line was used, workers in a factory had to be specialized to streamline and speed up production. The division is used not only in junior positions such as production line works but also at the top management level. That is why we have so many titles for top executives, such as CFO, COO, and CIO, in specific areas.

Logistics

All of us have limited resources, especially time. How to optimize the use of resources becomes one of the biggest problems that corporations and organizations have to solve.

Transportation-related companies, from local courier service companies to multinational logistic companies, have to find the shortest possible route that visits each client's position and returns to the distribution centre to minimize the delivery time and costs. It is a problem known as the Travelling Salesman Problem[51]. It will be a big task for them, even with the assistance of a supercomputer. It may not be a feasible task if they do not break down their delivery routes into a small number that they can handle.

Many corporations have the experience of having a bottleneck in their operations, and the retailers feel its pain the most. For example, the peak hours of restaurants are lunch hours and dinner time. Their patrons all rush into their establishments and look for seats, but not all of them are lucky. Some of them may have to wait for more than an hour, and eventually, they

---

[51] "Travelling salesman problem", Wikipedia, last accessed August 28, 2020, https://en.wikipedia.org/wiki/Travelling_salesman_problem

would go somewhere else. A loss of revenue for those restaurants is the result.

"How should we improve the process so that we can have seats for all the customers?"

That is a common question asked by many restaurant owners, but it is not the correct question they should ask. We will talk about the importance of setting the right question for problem-solving in Chapter 8. The question should be: *How can we maximize our revenue* (for the discussion below, we do not ask *How can we maximize our profit*)?

Unless it is a franchise restaurant, there are many ways to solve this problem. First of all, revenue does not necessarily come from sit-down patrons; it can be from take-out or delivery customers. Take-out and delivery have another benefit; if it is a pre-ordered take-out or delivery, the chef can prepare them in advance to avoid peak-hour problems.

Many restaurants offer morning and afternoon menus at discounted prices to attract people to come to their restaurants during their off-peak hours. Some of them, and some retailers as well, offer promotions on Wednesday as it is the day with the lowest sales during the week. Some restaurants divide their business hours into several slots and use apps and websites to let patrons reserve their tables for a single time slot. Such apps will also enable other patrons to see how full the restaurant will be in all time slots so that they can avoid peak time. The overall trick is to divide customers or time into different categories and manage them with different strategies.

Unit Price

I seldom do grocery shopping alone. One day, I was in a supermarket buying fruits and vegetables, and

I wanted to buy some raw almonds. I used to buy bottled roasted almonds as snacks. All of a sudden, I wanted to roast them myself as they would be both healthier and fresher.

When I picked some almonds from the big canister and put them into the plastic bag they provided, I noticed that the price of the almonds was $1.99 per 100 grams. It was the first time that I came across something that was selling per 100 grams instead of per pound or kilogram. It looked not too expensive at all when the price of almonds was divided by a smaller unit. Selling at $1.99 per 100 grams is the same as selling at $9.03 per pound or $19.90 per kg. At that time, most of the stores were selling almonds for only around $9 per pound or $13 per kg. That store selling $1.99 per 100-gram looked like a lower price than other stores, but it was, in fact, much higher.

That explains why more and more car dealerships advertise their leasing or financing rates per week. When the traditional method of calculation is per month, and you do it per week, your price will look like just 1/4 of the monthly rate. When it comes to real estate, many realtors would tell you that paying $5,000 more for a house is nothing because the extra monthly mortgage payment per year is not much. If you calculate it per day, it is less than the price of a cup of coffee. The realtor who helped me buy my first house told me the same. One thing I did not tell him was that I did not drink coffee at that age.

We cannot divide a house into portions and sell it separately, but we can divide the time of the ownership. That is the concept of time-sharing. If a cottage is worth $200,000 and we sell a time slot at $10,000 for one week's usage, this will be very attractive to the cottage goers. First, the price is only 5% of the value, and secondly, one week is the average time people will spend on a cottage per year.

However, it is a big leap in profit for the developers, as they divide the ownership by 52 weeks, with two weeks reserved for maintenance. In other words, when they sell a week of ownership at $10,000, the total revenue from that cottage is $500,000, which is 2.5 times the original value. That is an example of changing the unit price from per cottage to per week's ownership. An alternative method is to use a corporation to hold the cottage and sell its shares to people who want to co-own a cottage.

Mosaic

The stained glass of the churches is beautiful and iconic. Although they have over one thousand years of history[52], they are not the original design.

A Mosaic *is a coherent pattern or image in which each component element is built up from small regular or irregular pieces of substances such as stone, glass or ceramic,* which have more than 5,000 years of history[53]. The stained glass windows found in churches are actually a form of Mosaic.

It is a difficult task to build up an image or pattern with grains of glass or stones, but it will be much easier if we do it the other way – breaking down a big piece into small pieces.

Many years ago, a colleague of mine had a small round glass plate that he used as a mug cover. It was

---

[52] "Stained glass", Wikipedia, last accessed August 28, 2020, https://en.wikipedia.org/wiki/Stained_glass
[53] "Mosaic", Wikipedia, last accessed August 28, 2020, https://en.wikipedia.org/wiki/Mosaic

just a flat piece of glass plate, so it could only cover the mug but was easy to slip away. As expected, he broke it after using it for just a few weeks. I asked him to give the broken pieces to me to make a mosaic planet.

There were five big fragments, and I put them on five different trays. I further broke each fragment into smaller pieces one by one and ignored the crumbs. Once the first big fragment was done, I painted the small pieces with different colours and put them back to their original shape by using my puzzle-playing techniques. The second, third, fourth and last big fragments were all done in the same way. With the space left by taking out the crumbs, the final product was a perfect mosaic made by using the Reduction technique.

Multi-tools

In the development of the pocketknife, the designers used both Colouring and Reduction techniques. The first pocketknife is a small knife that can be put in a pocket[54] with a foldable handle added to it so that the knife can fit inside the hollow handle. Later, some pocketknives were made with two blades attached to both ends of the handle.

Since it is so convenient to put a pocketknife in the pocket, more tools are added to its body to make a multi-tool that has different types of tools. Screwdrivers, scissors, can openers, bottle openers, pliers, saws, and almost every type of tool have been diminished and added to a multi-tool.

Balloons

---

[54] "Pocketknife", Wikipedia, last accessed August 28, 2020, https://en.wikipedia.org/wiki/Pocketknife

Although hydrogen[55] was discovered in 1671 and is known as the lightest substance on earth, it was not used to obtain buoyancy for transportation purposes until 1783. The first balloon which carried passengers was a hot air balloon[56] made a couple of months before the hydrogen balloon was made[57].

Flying is a dream for many people, especially kids. However, riding a flying balloon at that time was not as affordable as today's first-class air ticket. Therefore, after the first latex balloon[58] was made in the 1920s, people filled the latex balloons with hydrogen gas to sell them as toys.

The kids overwhelmingly welcomed the little flying balloons. One of my summer jobs was selling flying aluminum foil balloons with cartoon characters on them. We could sell over 500 balloons per day even though the price for one balloon was $5, well over the cost of a meal at a fast-food restaurant at that time.

Rifles

Many people thought the concepts of a cannon and cannonball were created by enlarging a rifle and bullets because bullets and cannonballs were both solid metal balls at that time. Actually, it is the other way[59].

[55] "Hydrogen", Wikipedia, last accessed August 28, 2020, https://en.wikipedia.org/wiki/Hydrogen
[56] "Hot air balloon", Wikipedia, last accessed August 28, 2020, https://en.wikipedia.org/wiki/Hot_air_balloon
[57] "Gas balloon", Wikipedia, last accessed August 28, 2020, https://en.wikipedia.org/wiki/Gas_balloon
[58] "Toy balloon", Wikipedia, last accessed August 28, 2020, https://en.wikipedia.org/wiki/Toy_balloon
[59] "History of the firearm", Wikipedia, last accessed August 28, 2020, https://en.wikipedia.org/wiki/History_of_the_firearm

The cannon was invented in the twelfth century[60], and the rifle was invented in Europe during the fifteenth century[61]. A rifle is, actually, a diminished version of a cannon for easy carry by soldiers. A more compact firearm, a handgun, was consequently produced. The concept is like diminishing a desktop computer into a laptop and then into a tablet.

Tablets

Some people say that tablets are larger versions of smartphones (modified by the Enlargement technique), while others say they are mini versions of laptops (modified by the Reduction technique). I would say that they are modified by both techniques.

When the first tablet was made and promoted in the market, many people teased its size and limited functionality. They put several cell phones of that manufacturer together and tied them with tapes to tease that it was just a bigger cell phone with no added value. With other developments such as apps, data storage, and chips, the functions of tablets are now comparable to those of smartphones and notebook computers.

Memo Pad

The Reduction technique applies not only to high-tech products but also to common consumer products.

Although paperless and e-copy are the trends, memo pads are still in demand because they are always handy as you do not have to turn your computer on and wait for it to start. Moreover, it is inexpensive, so you can leave a memo pad at any place that is convenient

---

[60] "History of cannon", Wikipedia, last accessed August 28, 2020, https://en.wikipedia.org/wiki/History_of_cannon

[61] "Rifle", Wikipedia, last accessed August 28, 2020, https://en.wikipedia.org/wiki/Rifle

for you to use it. Inside your car, on your desk, or on the night table without worrying about any radiation.

Memo pads have many sizes, from full legal or letter size to smaller than four by four inches. The smallest memo pad (not sticky notes) that I had used was just the size of a business card. The small ones are usually used as promotional items with the advertiser's message on them.

The offset printing houses have to cut papers from large pieces to fit their customers' required sizes. One of the commonly used sizes is called Pliego[62]; its dimension is 70 cm by 100 cm. When the large pieces are cut into a letter or legal size, the edges to be cut are up to a few inches wide. Some printing houses will cut the residues into small squares to make memo pads for sale.

Miniatures

Making a cellphone or television is a challenging job as it involves high-end technologies. Making their display model is an easier task. Miniatures are good examples.

Interestingly, you do not have to reduce the size of the subject to the extreme possible limit to get the best result. That is, smaller may not be better. For example, if someone gives you an Eiffel Tower[63] keychain, you may not be excited enough to take a photo with it. However, when you go to a miniature park and see a mini Eiffel Tower in your size, you would love to take a photo with it.

---

[62] "Paper size", Wikipedia, last accessed August 28, 2020, https://en.wikipedia.org/wiki/Paper_size
[63] "Eiffel Tower", Wikipedia, last accessed August 28, 2020, https://en.wikipedia.org/wiki/Eiffel_Tower

Just like using the Enlargement technique to set world records, one can use the Reduction technique to set the smallest record. It is difficult to make a small drone, but it is easier to make a small pair of scissors that may set a world record.

Clocks and Watches

The ancient time-telling devices, such as sundials and water clocks[64], were usually huge and immobile. Even after the first mechanical clock was invented, the sizes of clocks were very large until spring-driven clocks were made during the fifteenth century[65]. With the newer technology, people started making smaller clocks and eventually, pocket watches evolved from portable spring-driven clocks[66]. As the size gets smaller and smaller, mechanical wristwatches were produced. With the invention of electronic quartz watches and digital watches, the size of a watch can be small enough to fit into a ring.

Now, a clock can be an 'intangible' one by using software to tell time, such as the system clock[67] or using the clock at the server and synchronizing the end unit to tell the accurate time. While the clock itself is getting smaller and smaller, the display screen has a limit. Actually, many timekeeping devices have an option for the user to adjust the size of the display clock.

Portable Equipment

---

[64]   "History of timekeeping devices", Wikipedia, last accessed August 28, 2020, https://en.wikipedia.org/wiki/History_of_timekeeping_devices
[65]   "Clock", Wikipedia, last accessed August 28, 2020, https://en.wikipedia.org/wiki/Clock
[66]   "Watch", Wikipedia, last accessed August 28, 2020, https://en.wikipedia.org/wiki/Watch
[67]   "System time", Wikipedia, last accessed August 28, 2020, https://en.wikipedia.org/wiki/System_time

If a piece of equipment can be disassembled and reassembled easily or simply diminished, it may be produced as a portable one or a compact one.

Can a house be portable? Maybe a tent is the answer to it. If not, then maybe a recreational vehicle is. Foldable bicycles and foldable guitars are based on the same logic – detaching the framework or skeleton to make the equipment portable or more compact. In the military, big structures such as barracks and bridges are all portable.

Chapter 5: Transposition

Transposition means substitution, a change of role, a change of presentation, a change of position of thinking or a change in how an idea is applied. The following examples may give you some insights into how to use the technique of Transposition to get creative ideas; some of them used other techniques in addition to the Transposition technique to improve the old ideas.

Subject Matter Expert

For some time, I was hired by a company as a Subject Matter Expert (SME) to write and review its articles. Because of the technical complexities, the company had a quality assurance procedure requiring that every article be peer-reviewed by at least two SMEs.

Honestly speaking, some of the fellow SMEs did not have the competency to do their jobs. They were hired just because they had decades of experience in the field. Some of them had no relevant academic degrees or professional training in the field. What was even worse was that their so-called professional experience included some bad habits and outdated knowledge.

One day, a series of emails were exchanged after I had made some content suggestions for something that one of my fellow SMEs wrote. After some correspondence, I sensed that he was not happy because he felt that I had stepped on his toes. He indicated that additional comments would not be accepted unless there were blatant mistakes. He wanted to make sure that his work would be approved as long as the work was not wrong. In other words, the quality of our work was unimportant. To exaggerate his thinking, it was akin to him writing a mathematics book about calculus but only including the content of simple arithmetic, addition, subtraction, multiplication and division. As long as there was no mistake in the context, we must approve it.

My problem was: *How can I improve the quality of our work without spoiling our relationship?*

I used the Transposition technique to change our roles. I proposed to him to let me draft the articles first and let him be the "Lead SME" to do the review and final approval. Because of the title "Lead SME", he was pleased to accept such a suggestion. Since I was much more knowledgeable than him, there were not many changes he could make. Furthermore, because I was more open-minded than him and accepted suggestions for changes, both the quality and speed of writing and review improved with this switch of our roles.

Giant Aquarium

The idea of building a huge aquarium is a challenge to many architects because the pressure of a million litres of water can easily break the glass. It is like building a huge dam using glass as the main structural material. This problem cannot be easily solved even if we use the strongest strengthened glass to build it.

Take a standard-size aquarium as an example. We, the humans, use aquariums to appreciate aquatic life by viewing them through glasses. The aquatic life, on the other hand, also watches the humans outside the aquarium. The only difference is that we are in a much bigger space than they are. In other words, we are not confined in a space, but they are. When we use a submarine to appreciate the natural marine life under the sea, the roles are exchanged. We are confined in a small tube, and the marine life is free.

Therefore, we can solve the huge aquarium challenge by switching roles. It is because it does not matter who is watching whom as long as they are viewing each other through the glass. Instead of using a large glass container to confine the aquatic life, we can use a smaller glass container to confine humans.

Underwater glass tunnels[68] are built inside huge concrete aquariums to serve the purpose of viewing aquatic life through unblocked glass walls. Many giant aquariums consist of two connected concrete structures, a large water container and a small viewing building around the container, and they are separated by walls with big glass windows for viewing purposes.

We may say these solutions did not use the technique of Transposition but the techniques of Enlargement and Reduction together. We multiply the volume of the aquarium and diminish the viewing space of the visitors.

Immigration

Canada is a great place for new immigrants. Since the 1970s, Canada has received hundreds of thousands of immigrants each year[69] from all over the world under four categories: Family, Economic, Protected person or Refugee, and Humanitarian or other[70].

---

[68] "Shark tunnel", Wikipedia, last accessed August 28, 2020,
      https://en.wikipedia.org/wiki/Shark_tunnel
[69] "History of immigration to Canada", Wikipedia, last accessed August 28, 2020,
      https://en.wikipedia.org/wiki/History_of_immigration_to_Canada
[70] "Immigration to Canada", Wikipedia, last accessed August 28, 2020,
      https://en.wikipedia.org/wiki/Immigration_to_Canada

A friend of mine was interested in migrating to Canada from Hong Kong in the 1990s. Among those four categories, the only possible one that he could be qualified for was to apply as a skilled worker under the Economic category. However, although there were many kinds of jobs that could qualify a person to immigrate to Canada, his job was not on the list.

He worked for a bank as an officer responsible for mortgages and commercial loans. Bank employees or personal bankers were not listed as qualified skilled workers, so he told me he would not proceed. I referred him to an immigration consultant for a professional review. What the consultant found out was that he should not have limited his job title to Bank Officer; that was why he could not find the relevant skilled worker class on the list. The Canadian government would not limit skilled workers to be in a particular industry. For example, the category Management was a general class and would not be stipulated to banks, real estate companies or any particular field. My friend thought he was only a bank employee, like the tellers sitting and working at a branch; that was why he could not find the right skilled worker class to apply for immigration.

After talking to the immigration consultant, my friend applied for immigration under the working class Marketing and Sales and was approved. He continued his career as a personal banker in Canada right after landing, and it has been more than 25 years now.

While job positions can be described differently under different functions, products and ideas can be presented differently using different aspects and presentation skills, too.

Luxury Goods

What are luxury goods? Although there are different opinions, basically all their prices are high. Some say they are goods for which demand increases more than proportionally as income rises so that expenditures on the goods become a greater proportion of overall spending[71]. Some say they must be scarce and have high prices, and the scarcity of the goods can be natural or artificial[72].

Luxury goods are not just expensive, and their profit margins are also high. If one can make a luxury product, it will be a good idea to make and sell it. The most important factor of luxury goods is that they must be scarce, but the scarcity can be artificial. That gives the manufacturers some room for manipulation.

In Chapter 4, we talked about clocks and watches. The new technologies make them not only small but also very accurate. After the invention of the quartz clock[73], accurate and affordable quartz watches have also been produced. It hurt the mechanical watch[74] manufacturers who had dominated the market for years, especially the Swiss luxury watch manufacturers.

The Swiss watchmakers have been proud of their craftsmanship and called their watchmaking process the art of precision. However, mechanical watches cannot compete with quartz watches in terms of accuracy and price. Therefore, there was a significant decline in the

---

[71] "Luxury goods", Wikipedia, last accessed August 28, 2020, https://en.wikipedia.org/wiki/Luxury_goods

[72] "Superior good", Wikipedia, last accessed August 28, 2020, https://en.wikipedia.org/wiki/Superior_good

[73] "Quartz clock", Wikipedia, last accessed August 28, 2020, https://en.wikipedia.org/wiki/Quartz_clock

[74] "Mechanical watch", Wikipedia, last accessed August 28, 2020, https://en.wikipedia.org/wiki/Mechanical_watch

Swiss watchmaking industry starting in the late 1970s.[75] To react, one Swiss watchmaker produced a series of plastic body quartz watches that were more trendy and affordable than their traditional mechanical watches, which was a huge success.

Moreover, they started focusing on the high-end market and promoted their watches as luxury as jewelry instead of just timekeeping devices. That is similar to the case of pen manufacturers in Chapter 1.

Once a luxury brand has been established, it is easy to manipulate the position of products. A cotton T-shirt without any special cutting and design can only be sold for a dollar or two. However, if a luxury product manufacturer prints a big trademark of their brand on the same T-shirt, then it can be sold for twenty or thirty dollars easily.

Insurance

If your luxury sports car is stolen and burnt, the compensation you will get from your insurance company may exceed one million dollars. Such an amount may be more than the total amount of premiums that you will pay the insurance company in your whole life. That is why buying an insurance policy for something important is a good idea, even though it is not mandatory to buy one.

On the other hand, if you were an insurance company that insured the first US satellite to be launched by NASA and the launch failed, the satellite exploded with the rocket, you would have lost money even with reinsurance bought. The reason is that there was only one client (insurance policy) of this kind, so

---

[75] "Quartz crisis", Wikipedia, last accessed August 28, 2020, https://en.wikipedia.org/wiki/Quartz_crisis

there is no premium contributed by other clients to cover your compensation. You may have the reinsurance, but it may not be full coverage, and it also costs you the premium to buy such reinsurance, so it may still cause a loss to you.

The case will change if there are enough clients in the pool, especially for mandatory insurance such as automobile insurance and professional errors and omissions insurance. It is because if the insurance company has to pay out compensation, say $10 million, they will make sure that the total premium payments from other insured clients are over $10 million. In other words, the premiums will be increased to protect the insurance company if the claims go up.

It is a win-win situation to make sure that all insured clients will get compensation because the insurance company will not go bankrupt by being able to charge enough premiums from other clients to pay for that compensation. In the eyes of those people who got compensated, they are getting benefits from the insurance company. From the eyes of people who have not filed any claim, they are paying their insurance premium for 'nothing'. That is, compensations are given to a small group of clients only, and the rest will be responsible for paying such compensations.

Such a concept is used in other industries, such as restaurants and retail stores. For the buffet or all-you-can-eat restaurants, there may be some customers who can eat a lot, and the cost of the food they consume is well over the price they paid. However, the majority of customers eat well under the costs, so those restaurants still can generate good profits from there.

Some retailers offer hassle-free return policies so that the customers do not have to give any reason to return their merchandise and get a refund. That may create a loss from that transaction but will create a good reputation and get more customers to shop at their stores. Both of these two examples are transposed from the strategy that insurance companies use.

Seminars

Many business-related non-fiction authors will provide seminars to corporations, non-profit organizations and government institutions to share with the audience their views, theories or methodologies that have been talked about in their books. I do the same, especially for this book[76]. The reason why we offer seminars to talk about a book is that we think like the audience to find out the benefits for the audience.

The first question that many people may ask is: *Why don't they buy the book to read but attend the seminar?* Some of them did, and many of them won't. It is like some films that are based on a novel. Some people like to read the book but not to watch the movie, some people like the other way, and some will do both. Reading a book is more flexible than watching a movie, especially if we have to watch the movie in the theatre. However, it is more time-consuming to read a book as it is more detailed than a movie. A movie is like a summary of a book but may have omitted some of the scenes.

We talked about paperless books in Chapter 2. Seminars of this type are similar to paperless books, but when we transpose a book into a seminar, we need to add more value to it.

First of all, it saves time. For the audience, spending a few hours listening to a summary of a book

---

[76] "Certificate in Creative Problem-solving", Fox College of Business, last accessed August 28, 2020, http://www.differentialcogitation.com/courses.html

saves them time. Secondly, it allows the author to apply the theories that may not be available in the book to that particular organization. Lastly, a seminar has a Q and A section that enables the audience to ask specific questions related to their jobs or personal lives.

Laziness

It is important to know what your clients and customers think. Most inventions or new products are based on consumer needs. One of the biggest consumer needs is to save the labour force. More directly, consumers are lazy and want some help. For some people who do not want to read, going to a seminar or listening to an audiobook is an excellent alternative to reading a book.

Some people like to dine out just because they are lazy and do not want to cook. Some are too busy at work and do not have time to cook, especially those who live alone. Some are the working groups in the company who go out to dine after their overtime work. However, some of these people may not even have time to go to the restaurant, so pick-up orders are not an option, and delivery is their only choice.

Traditionally, most restaurants, except the franchise fast foods, do not offer delivery service. Even if they do, your location may be out of their boundaries. Third-party food delivery service companies, therefore, appeared. The revenue in the online food delivery segment in China alone is projected to be more than US$51 billion in 2020[77].

There are two types of food delivery services: 'hidden' and 'stand-alone'. Some companies provide

---

[77] "Online Food Delivery", Statista, last accessed August 28, 2020,
https://www.statista.com/outlook/374/117/online-food-delivery/china

delivery services to restaurants in a way that the customers do not know who the delivery company is. They order their food directly from the restaurants, and the restaurant may assign its delivery jobs to more than one service provider. That is the 'hidden' type.

Another type is 'stand-alone'. This type of service provider has its own website for customers to order food from the restaurants listed with them[78]. It does not matter which restaurants you want to order; as long as they are associated with that service provider, you can go to the website of that service provider to order your food.

---

[78]   "Online food ordering", Wikipedia, last accessed August 28, 2020, https://en.wikipedia.org/wiki/Online_food_ordering

Chapter 6: Mapping

All ideas are based on existing facts or ideas. So far, we have learned how to change the existing ones by using the techniques mentioned above. For those ideas or products that have been created but no one has used them yet, there may be good opportunities to use them if you can map them to the right application. Some existing ideas may be good for solving your problem, but you have to modify them to apply to your situation. That is, it is a matching game – use the right idea or product in the right way.

Typically, the five Ws and one H questions technique will be used to set some questions that you have to answer. Although not all of the Ws have to be used, you should try to ask as many relevant questions as possible. Questions that should be asked may include:

Who will use this idea?

Who will be affected by this idea?

What can this idea create?

What are the characteristics of this idea?

When will this idea be applied to get the best result?

When will people use this idea?

Where should this idea be promoted?

Where should we apply this idea?

Why should people use this idea?

Why is this idea a good alternative?

How can we apply this idea?

How can we modify this idea?

The following examples may give you some insights into how to use the Mapping technique to get creative ideas; some of them used other techniques in addition to the Mapping technique to improve the old ideas.

Sticky Notes

Sticky notes require the use of a low-tack, reusable, and pressure-sensitive adhesive to attach, remove, and re-post the notes without leaving residue. Such adhesive was invented and patented, but it was initially a failed invention. It was a failed product when the scientist attempted to develop a super-strong adhesive, but he produced a low-tack one instead[79].

With a failed product, the inventor spent five years promoting his product and trying to convince his colleagues to sell it to the market. The problem was that he got a product with no application, as everyone would look for a high-tack one when they looked for an adhesive to use. Eventually, one of his colleagues found a way to produce sticky notes, which became one of the best-selling products of their company.

---

[79] "Post-it Note", Wikipedia, last accessed August 28, 2020, https://en.wikipedia.org/wiki/Post-it_Note

If the inventor had used the five Ws and one H questions approach, he should have spent less time finding out the application of his new product. Below are the questions that could have been asked:

Question: Why should people use this low-tack adhesive?

Answer: They do not want the items to be permanently stuck together.

Possible Outcomes: Things that are not permanently placed, such as for an exhibition.

Question: Where can the low-tack adhesive be applied?

Answer: To apply it on some surfaces that are easy to stick. Rough surfaces are not suitable. The object has to be light in weight as the adhesive cannot hold heavy items.

Possible Outcomes: Paper, films (at that time, cameras used plastic films), micro-films, plastic bags.

Question: What are the benefits of this adhesive?

Answer: It will not cause damage to any item when we remove it.

Possible Outcomes: To be used on some materials that are easily damaged when strong glue is removed, such as paper, painted wood, rubbers and soft plastics.

Question: What can be created by using this low-tack adhesive?

Answer: An adhesive by itself or as part of another finished product.

Possible Outcome: A glue that sticks photos or notes on the wall without damaging the paint.

If they had kept on asking such kinds of questions, they should have produced sticky notes within months after the invention of the adhesive.

Hook-and-loop fastener

Similar to the adhesive that was invented prior to the sticky notes, the hook-and-loop fastener was created after the natural 'adhesive' had been found.

The hook-and-loop fastener was conceived by Swiss engineer George de Mestral. The idea came to him just one day after returning from a hunting trip with his dog when he found something that kept sticking to his clothes and his dog's fur. He examined them and noted they had hooks that could catch on anything with a loop, such as clothing and animal fur. He then invented the hook-and-loop fastener by producing the hooks and loops in nylon[80].

We did not know whether George de Mestral had used the five Ws and one H questions to explore the idea or not, but such a questioning process can definitely help you get a good product invented if you come across a similar opportunity.

---

[80] "Hook-and-loop fastener", Wikipedia, last accessed August 28, 2020, https://en.wikipedia.org/wiki/Hook-and-loop_fastener

High-speed Train

The engineers of the newest high-speed trains were interviewed. Before making the trains possible, the first thing they had to do was to make the experimental model train and track possible. Their model train and track were proportional to the real one, including the tunnel. Of course, the speed was also the same as the real one, which exceeded 450 km/h.

One of their challenges was how to stop the model train at such a high speed. Unlike a real train, the model train had no driver to apply the brakes, and it was too expensive and complicated to install a remote braking system inside the model train. The engineers tried using buffers at the end of the track, but the model train was travelling like a real bullet; the buffer was either too weak to stop the train or too strong that it broke the train.

One of the lead engineers solved the problem when he was playing with a toy with his kid. He noticed a natural force that had been discovered thousands of years ago might help him – the magnetic force. When placing a set of magnets on the wall built at the end of the track and another set at the tip of the train with the like poles facing each other, the repelling force could slow down the train without physically touching the body of the train. Two other sets of magnets were placed under the train and at the end of the track, with their unlike poles facing each other. The attraction between the two sets of magnets would increase the friction between the train and the track, so the train would also be forced to slow down. With the magnetic forces, the model train could be stopped untouched so that the train would not be damaged.

The engineer successfully mapped the magnetic force to the braking force in the model train.

Steam Engine

Similar to magnetic force, steam is also a kind of natural energy that inventors discovered and applied. After Thomas Savery[81] had invented the first commercially used steam-powered device in 1698, the mechanisms of steam-powered engines were further improved by Thomas Newcomen[82] and James Watt[83], and the improved steam-powered engine was the key to the first industrial revolution. However, steam-driven devices, known as an aeolipile, were invented as early as the first century[84]. If people could use the five Ws and one H questions technique to improve the aeolipile, the first industrial revolution might have happened more than one thousand years earlier.

Lease-to-own

Vehicle leasing is a very common alternative to buying a vehicle with a conventional car loan. It is normally offered by a new car dealership with a leasing term of three or four years. After the leasing term period, you can either return the vehicle to the dealership or purchase it for its residual value.

For the same length of the term, say four years, the lease payment is lower than the loan payment. However, you have to pay for the residual value to buy back the vehicle if you want the vehicle after the leasing term. For a car loan, the debt will be paid off at

---

[81] "Thomas Savery", Wikipedia, last accessed August 28, 2020, https://en.wikipedia.org/wiki/Thomas_Savery

[82] "Thomas Newcomen", Wikipedia, last accessed August 28, 2020, https://en.wikipedia.org/wiki/Thomas_Newcomen

[83] "James Watt", Wikipedia, last accessed August 28, 2020, https://en.wikipedia.org/wiki/James_Watt

[84] "Aeolipile", Wikipedia, last accessed August 28, 2020, https://en.wikipedia.org/wiki/Aeolipile

the end of the installment period, and you do not have to pay for your vehicle anymore.

Such a lease-to-own option to help people own a vehicle is mapped to other industries, such as real estate. Some developers offer lease-to-own options to people who cannot afford to pay the down payment. The monthly rent will be inflated a little bit so that part of it will be saved by the developer as the tenants' down payment when they want to buy the property after a lease term of, say, five years.

In commercial real estate, similar lease-to-own arrangements are offered to corporations to own properties in "installments" without increasing their liabilities, such as via synthetic leases[85].

Trial and Error

Since this Mapping technique is used to modify an existing idea or apply it to your situation, the modification may have to be adjusted by trial and error.

There is no unique method to set the five Ws and one H questions. It is like making alloy steel;[86] although we know that they are iron alloyed with carbon, other elements such as manganese, nickel, chromium, molybdenum, vanadium, silicon, and boron are also added. Their percentages are not fixed, and you have to find the right combination to produce the type of alloy steel that you want. Other elements, including aluminum, cobalt, copper, cerium, niobium, titanium, tungsten, tin, zinc, lead, and zirconium, may also be added, although they are less commonly used.

---

[85] "Synthetic lease", Wikipedia, last accessed August 28, 2020, https://en.wikipedia.org/wiki/Synthetic_lease
[86] "Alloy steel", Wikipedia, last accessed August 28, 2020, https://en.wikipedia.org/wiki/Alloy_steel

The type of elements and the quantity of them to be added all depend on the type of alloy steel you want to produce. You may need a kind of alloy steel that is corrosion-resistant, hard, wear-resistant, tough or else, so you may have to try numerous combinations of elements and test the results.

Free Product or Service

Giving out free products or services is a good way to promote them, especially when they are new products or services. However, the free sample should be small in amount, and the free service should be short in time. Otherwise, the costs will be too much as they are given out free of charge.

Some scenarios in the freebies are given out 'conditionally', such as 'buy one get one free'. In other words, it is a kind of discount. 'Buy one get one free' is 50% off, 'buy two get one free' is 33% off and so on. This kind of promotion is good for products with a relatively high profit margin as they can offer a higher discount. For services and other products with low margins, this kind of promotion cannot be copied directly, and you need to learn the best method from trial and error or other people's success stories.

Many financial institutions offer free trials to attract people to use their services. Three decades ago, they would waive your annual fee for the first year so that you could try their credit cards free of charge for one year. On top of waiving the annual fee, the financial institutions might give out presents when the customers apply for their cards. They would have to pay commissions to the salespersons, too, plus the cards might have other benefits such as cash rebates, travel points, etc. However, many people applied for their cards, got the present (and the salespersons got their commission), used it for one year, and earned the points or cash rebates, but they cancelled their cards right before the end of the first year. Those financial institutions suffered considerable losses from such promotions.

Some of them learned a lesson from there and changed their strategy. They offered the same terms and conditions as before, except that the annual fee would only be waived in the second year. In this way, the customers must pay for the first year's fee, and the financial institutions would not lose money even if the customers cancel their cards after the first year.

Similar promotions were done in the real estate industry during the recession time. In the mid-1990s, the real estate market in North America was at the bottom, and many commercial landlords offered free base rent to attract tenants. All the landlords wanted was to have the tenants pay for the operating costs such as the realty taxes, maintenance and insurance. Many landlords offer a free rent period for one to two years, and the tenants would start paying market rent after that period.

As you can foresee, many tenants took advantage of this type of offer and tried their luck. During the recession, many people were laid off, and many of them became entrepreneurs. Some of them took advantage of the landlords and tried to develop their business within the first two years. If they failed, they would close their business or even go bankrupt.

Some of the landlords used the "buy 12 get one free" approach and offered one-month free rent to the tenants for every year they committed to the lease term. That is, if a tenant commits a 5-year lease term, the landlord will give that tenant five months free rent. If the tenant commits a 10-year lease term, there will be ten months' free rent. The problem was the landlords gave the free rent period at the beginning of the lease term. Again, some aggressive tenants took advantage of free rent and tried their luck in their new business; most of them committed to ten-year leases and got almost one year of free rent to start their business.

Through these 'trial and error' experiences, most landlords will only offer free rent at the end of the lease term or the end of each year. So, for example, if a landlord offers one month of free rent per year committed to the lease, and a tenant commits to a ten-year lease, then the landlord will give the ten months free rent at the end of the ten-year term (the last ten months will be free at the end of the ten years). The alternative is to give the tenant one month of free rent at the end of every year (one month of free rent will be given after 11 months of rent is paid).

Although there are failures in the credit card and real estate industries, I still come across some companies that offer their annual fees waived in the first year or free rent at the beginning of the lease term. Clearly, those companies did not pay attention to history and, hence, failed to learn a lesson. Trial and error may not have to be done by you; they can be done by other people.

Chapter 7: Dimension

When no new idea can be created, sometimes it is worth reviewing the old ideas, especially those proposed by your colleagues before but have never been used. Dimension is a technique to apply an existing idea from one field to another field, from one dimension to another dimension. It is not a good idea now, but it may be a good idea in the future. It is not a good idea for this project, but it may be a good idea for another project. Basically, the idea is copied without any change or just with a little change.

The following examples may give you some insights into how to use the Dimension technique to get creative ideas by copying the existing ones or improving the old ideas.

Fashion Design – Change of Time

Some say *if you live long enough, you will probably see the fashion trends of your youth cycling back into popularity*[87]. That is so true – based on my personal experience, especially the formal dresses.

Unlike cars, aeroplanes and computers, the difficulty of fashion design is that the function and performance of most clothing are not as important as their appearance. The changes that can be made to garments are very limited because there are basic items

---

[87] "The 20 Year Trend Cycle: What Is Next?", Fashion Industry Broadcast, last updated March 9, 2016, https://fashionindustrybroadcast.com/2016/03/09/20-year-trend-cycle-next/

to be included, such as tops, pants (or skirts), and footwear.

Take men's suits as an example. A full set of men's suits has a shirt, jacket and trousers; traditionally, it has a waistcoat as well. Designs are bounded by this combination and have limited choices. The variations basically are two-piece or three-piece (without or with waistcoat), number of buttons used, single-breasted or double-breasted, have a handkerchief or not, use suspenders or belt, types of lapel cuts, etc. The trend 'recycles' after a period of time.

Movies and TV Programs – Change of Country

Most films and TV programs are the original creations of the directors or screenwriters, but many of them have copied the ideas or plots from others, especially from those in other countries or regions. Some of them bought the copyrights, but some of them did not.

One of my favourite movie series is the "Man with No Name Trilogy[88]" (also known as Dollars Trilogy[89]), which consists of three popular movies: *A Fistful of Dollars*, *For a Few Dollars More* and *The Good, the Bad and the Ugly*. Filmed in 1964, *A Fistful of Dollars* was allegedly a remake of the Japanese director Akira Kurosawa's 1961 film *Yojimbo[90]*. I watched both movies and basically, their plots are quite similar. The biggest difference is that *Yojimbo* happened in Japan during the final years of the Edo period in

---

[88] "Man with No Name", Wikipedia, last accessed August 28, 2020, https://en.wikipedia.org/wiki/Man_with_No_Name

[89] "Dollars Trilogy", Wikipedia, last accessed August 28, 2020, https://en.wikipedia.org/wiki/Dollars_Trilogy

[90] "A Fistful of Dollars", Wikipedia, last accessed August 28, 2020, https://en.wikipedia.org/wiki/A_Fistful_of_Dollars

1860, and people used Samurai swords to fight. *A Fistful of Dollars* happened in the wild west of the USA, and people used guns.

Another successful movie that is a licensed remake of an Asian film is *The Departed*[91], launched in 2006. It is a remake of the 2002 Hong Kong film *Infernal Affairs*[92]. Except for a tweak in the ending, the only difference between the two is the background of the stories. One is in Hong Kong, and one is in the USA.

Many reality shows and TV programs are reproduced in other countries, such as *Who Wants to Be a Millionaire?*[93], *America's Got Talent*[94] and *MasterChef*[95]. While most local TV stations paid franchise or copyright fees to remake an overseas TV program, many TV dramas copied the plots and character modelling of overseas programs without authorization and are condemned by the audience. Copying an idea may involve copyright or patent issues, so we have to be cautious.

Cigarette – Change of Three-dimensional Space

A tobacco manufacturer wanted to produce a new brand of cigarettes, but they had already produced different brands of cigarettes with different favours, tar and nicotine levels. Moreover, the new division had a

---

[91] "The Departed", Wikipedia, last accessed August 28, 2020, https://en.wikipedia.org/wiki/The_Departed
[92] "Infernal Affairs", Wikipedia, last accessed August 28, 2020, https://en.wikipedia.org/wiki/Infernal_Affairs
[93] "Who Wants to Be a Millionaire?", Wikipedia, last accessed August 28, 2020, https://en.wikipedia.org/wiki/Who_Wants_to_Be_a_Millionaire%3F
[94] "America's Got Talent", Wikipedia, last accessed August 28, 2020, https://en.wikipedia.org/wiki/America%27s_Got_Talent
[95] "MasterChef", Wikipedia, last accessed August 28, 2020, https://en.wikipedia.org/wiki/MasterChef

limited budget for the advertisement, research and development of the new product, so they needed some gimmicks to promote it.

They eventually used different dimensions to produce a new brand – they increased the length of the cigarette without changing the overall size (volume). The length of the new cigarette was much longer than all other brands, but the diameter was smaller (thinner), so the amount of tobacco per cigarette was the same as other brands.

Such a long cigarette was a successful gimmick and created the noise. Moreover, many people thought there was more tobacco in it, and they could smoke it for a longer time because it was longer in size. It is simply not true.

Chocolates – Change of Shape

Similar to the cigarette manufacturer, two confectionery companies also played with the shape of their product and had a big success.

The first company made chocolate wafer cookies in the shape of a cigarette. It was so welcomed by the kids as they could imitate adult smoking. I was one of those kids that always asked my grandma to buy some. The idea of "cigarette cookies" was a huge success until some people criticized the company for promoting smoking to kids, including toddlers. As a result, the company kept the shape but advertised it as "finger cookies". Unfortunately, the sales revenue dropped, and it could not achieve the same level as before.

Another company made their chocolate in a triangular shape, and such a shape helped it stand out from all other brands and gained a big success.

Management Style – Change of Organizations

The top senior executives of a corporation are supposed to be capable of managing the company in the best shape regardless of what kind of business the company is. It is, therefore, crucial to hire experienced C-suite executives as they might have dealt with the situations and would be capable of duplicating the solutions from one company to another. In other words, management styles or techniques can be copied from one organization to another.

Kazuo Inamori[96] is the founder of Kyocera[97] and a successful entrepreneur in Japan. He designed a management system called Amoeba[98], which has been adopted by many corporations. Because of his excellent management skills, he was invited to take the Chief Executive Officer position at Japan Airlines in 2010, when the airline suffered steep financial losses[99]. After exiting bankruptcy, Japan Airlines also adopted Amoeba as their management system.

The Art of War – Change of Situations

If you wonder how many times an idea can be copied and applied to different situations, the *Art of Wars* will be the best answer. Although *The Art of War* was written around two thousand and five hundred years ago, it has valuable advice for everyone today.

Many people are misled by the name *"The Art of War";* it is a Chinese book more than a military treatise. While it contains military strategies, their

---

[96] "Kazuo Inamori", Wikipedia, last accessed August 28, 2020, https://en.wikipedia.org/wiki/Kazuo_Inamori

[97] "Kyocera", Wikipedia, last accessed August 28, 2020, https://en.wikipedia.org/wiki/Kyocera

[98] "Amoeba Management", Wikipedia, last accessed August 28, 2020, https://en.wikipedia.org/wiki/Amoeba_Management

[99] "Japan Airlines", Wikipedia, last accessed August 28, 2020, https://en.wikipedia.org/wiki/Japan_Airlines

applications are beyond the war fields[100]. Take one of the quotes from the book as an example. It says,

Winning one hundred victories in one hundred battles is not the aim of skill. To subdue the enemy without fighting is the acme of skill[101].

If a country has to fight in a battle, the war will cost them casualties even if they win. The best way to deal with the enemy is, therefore, to defeat them without going to battle. That is why superpowers such as the United States, Russia, and China are all equipped with nuclear weapons that are powerful enough to destroy the earth many times if they use those weapons. Instead of launching them, the missiles are mainly used to intimidate the rivals.

A price war is the same. No corporation wants to participate in a price war as it will lower its profit. However, the prerequisite to avoid a price war is that you are big enough so that the competitors know they cannot beat you with a price war. Therefore, big retailers often offer other value-added services to their stores rather than selling all their products at throat-cutting low prices. As we have talked about in Chapter 5, some of them offer hassle-free return and refund policies, and some of them offer free shipping for qualified orders online.

Another way to avoid price wars is to avoid head-on competition with rivals, especially those of comparable sizes. Many big retailers will ask their landlords to sign an exclusive use clause in their lease to protect their business. Such a clause asks the

---

[100] "The Art of War", Wikipedia, last accessed August 28, 2020, https://en.wikipedia.org/wiki/The_Art_of_War
[101] "Sun_Tzu", Wikiquote, last accessed August 28, 2020, https://en.wikiquote.org/wiki/Sun_Tzu

landlord to agree not to rent out any unit in the landlord's shopping centre to their competitors or any businesses offering the same kind of products or services. That will keep all rivals away so that they will not have head-on competition in the same shopping centre.

In some extreme cases, the merchant will rent a unit in another shopping centre nearby with the same type of exclusive clause signed. However, they will not open a store in that shopping centre as they do not want to compete with themselves. They just simply pay the rent without operating a store there. In this way, they can keep their rivals away in both shopping centres.

To conclude, new ideas are based on old ideas; it depends on how much percentage of a new idea is brand new. We should always pay attention to the existing matters, both natural and artificial, to broaden our visions. We can summarize all the creativity techniques by the popular Pablo Picasso[102] quote :

"When there's anything to steal, I steal".

---

[102] "Pablo Picasso", Wikiquote, last accessed August 28, 2020, https://en.wikiquote.org/wiki/Pablo_Picasso

Chapter 8: Goal Setting

Now, you have all the tools to get creative ideas and use them to solve problems. It is like you can drive a car freely and use the car to go to your destination. The next step is to know your destination, as you do not want to drive endlessly. That is, the next step is to find out the goal you want to achieve. Once our goal is set, we can use the reverse thinking technique[103] to find out the best route to achieve it, which will be discussed in the next chapter.

In any problem-solving task, we must identify and understand the problem first. Without a problem, we have nothing to solve. However, the problem actually depends on our goal. If we do not know our final goal or we do not set it correctly, even if we can solve the "problem", we may not solve the real problem or may miss a better alternative.

If a goal is set too broadly, then we may have too many possible solutions, which would not be good for the testing process. If a goal is too specific, then it limits the number of solutions.

Your goal sets the boundaries of your solutions for you. A broader goal gives you more room to work with so that you <u>don't have</u> to *think outside of the box* because you have a much bigger box. A goal that is too specific will limit not only the number of solutions but

---

[103] A process of problem-solving that to reveal to possible solutions by reviewing the routes from the goal back to the starting point instead of from the starting point to the goal.

also the possibility of achieving a better result. That is why setting a goal is the most important step in problem-solving. Otherwise, you may be solving a problem that is not bringing any benefit to you.

Goals and problems are related but may not be the same or may not be one-on-one. If the goal is to have more money, then the problem is *how to make more money?* If the goal is to have a faster computer, then the problem can be *how to make a faster computer*, *where to buy a faster computer*, or *how to make more money to buy a faster computer?*

Goal Setting

When we have a problem, we want to solve it. However, solving an existing problem may not be our real goal. The most important step in problem-solving is to have a lucidly defined problem. It is because if we want to find the best solution to the problem, we must define our problem well enough so that we will not exclude some possible solutions.

If we refine the problem by setting a higher or broader goal, we may end up with more and better solutions. Therefore, before we can apply the reverse thinking technique, the first step we must do is set our goal.

Discussing your objective with other people is a good way to find out the right goal, especially with people not involved in the project. Often, those people will give you unbiased opinions on how to broaden your target or clarify your goals. We may consider a few examples to illustrate how important it is to set the right goal.

Mistress

Let us take the hypothetical example of a lady whose husband is having an affair. That is, her problem is that her husband has a mistress. What will be her goal? One may say her goal is *to turn her husband's mistress away or make sure her husband has no mistress*. However, that is not the only goal you can set. That is also not the right goal. *Turning her husband's mistress away* is not good enough, as her husband may find another mistress later. *Ensuring her husband has no mistress* is not broad enough, as this goal will exclude some solutions to the problem, such as divorce.

The goal should be broader; it should be to *make sure she does not have a husband who has a mistress*. This goal includes the solution of being single. Having a divorce and then keeping a single status can serve the purpose of *not having a husband who has a mistress*.

If you do not perform a goal-setting process, you may still be able to find a solution to a problem by using traditional problem-solving methods; however, the outcome may not be the one that you desire or may not be the best one, as you may have missed some solutions.

Cell Phone Manufacturers

The first handheld cellular mobile phone was made in the early 1970s, weighing 2 kilograms and looked like the size of a brick. Since it was too heavy and bulky, many of those units were designed to be used inside vehicles, which could get an 'unlimited' power supply from the vehicle engine and battery. For years, manufacturers had been trying to reduce the size of mobile phones, effectively, "the smaller, the better".

If we limit the issue of cell phones to size only, then at the time, the goal of many cell phone manufacturers might be *to produce a smaller and lighter cell phone*. However, some of them noticed that even if the technologies at the time allowed them to shrink a cell phone to any size they wanted, there were limitations. The buttons and screen could not be too small. Therefore, the goal of the manufacturers should have been *to produce a cell phone with a comfortable size and weight to use.*

A Coffee Shop

More than two decades ago, a friend of mine wanted to open a coffee shop. He had everything ready – registered a trademark, leased a store, installed all the equipment and leasehold improvement, hired experienced employees and planned extensive promotional programs. Right before his grand opening, he showed me all his hard work and asked for my opinion.

"What is your goal?" I asked him.

"To make money, of course!" he answered shortly.

As setting the goal is the most important step in the Reverse Thinking process, I asked him more questions and found out his final goal was *to open several coffee shops one by one and eventually turn them into a franchise business.* I used the Reverse Thinking technique to help him by asking him how to achieve his goals, level by level. In the end, we found out that the main problem he had to solve was: *How can he differentiate his coffee shop from the others?* More precisely, *How can he stand out from the market leaders to capture some of their market shares?*

Once the problem is set, the next step is to find a route to use to help solve the problem. After reviewing every stage in the flow chart, I helped him solve this problem by applying the *Enlargement* tool, which is the case discussed in Chapter 3.

84

Beauty Pageant

A teenager told me that she would love to be a beauty pageant contestant to give herself more self-confidence. Ironically, she lacked the confidence to enroll in the beauty pageant that interested her, afraid of not even having an interview or getting eliminated in the very preliminary round.

Although there are many ways to increase our self-confidence level, she insisted that being qualified in a beauty pageant would be the most effective way to do so. The one she was interested in was the first and biggest nationwide beauty pageant, which explained her hesitation in registering. As I knew that there were at least three similar beauty pageants in Canada at the time, I helped her amend her goal after further conversations from *"to win the XXX beauty pageant"* to *"to be a finalist in one of the five beauty pageants we picked"*. Eventually, she fulfilled her dream and has become a more confident lady since then.

If we did not change her goal from *winning a particular beauty pageant* to *being a finalist in one of the several beauty pageants*, she could not have achieved her goal and consequently increased her confidence level.

A Detergent Manufacturer

The second-largest detergent company, which had 25% of market shares, wanted to improve its product to acquire more shares. Their goal was to *produce a better product* or to *acquire a greater market share*. They employed all the creative thinking techniques and invented a detergent with eight times greater cleaning power than the market leader at the time. It also applied the methods to promote its new product with creative advertisements. As a result, the market share of its new product increased to 40%, becoming the leader in that field.

However, every product in the market has also increased its cleaning power to double. It caused the total quantity of detergent sold to be reduced by 50%. The market revenue had decreased from $1,000 ml to $500 ml. Therefore, the corporate revenue was reduced from $250 ml to $200 ml.

Its product had been improved, market share had been increased, and the 'problem' was solved. However, the corporation's fundamental goal of increasing profits was not achieved. If the corporation had set its goal of increasing profits before launching its creative thinking problem-solving process, it should have been able to achieve this goal with the new product.

In other words, the corporation could have achieved its goal of higher profits by better defining its goal.

A Shampoo Manufacturer

Similar to the detergent manufacturer, a shampoo manufacturer wanted to increase its market share by improving its shampoo. Unlike detergent, the potency of shampoo can have harmful effects; the shampoo may hurt our hair and skin if its cleaning power is too strong. Therefore, the goal of a detergent manufacturer to create a better product can be *to produce a detergent with the highest cleaning power,* but this cannot be the case for a shampoo manufacturer. Instead, the goal of a better product for a shampoo producer can simply be *"to produce a better shampoo"*. While it is vague to have such a goal, it gives us a broader scope to define and achieve it.

A "better" shampoo to consumers can be one at a lower price, with a celebrity as the brand ambassador to show its luxury, or simply with better quality. A 2-in-1 formula, conditioner and shampoo was the solution to a 'better shampoo' decades ago. The topic "How to make a better shampoo" is discussed in Chapter 1.

Award-Winning Movies

The goal of the people in the movie industry is *to produce a good movie*. The question they should ask, therefore, when setting their goal is: What makes a good movie?

While some may say that it should be one of the highest-grossing movies or at least with a good box-office record, others may believe it should win some awards, such as the Academy Awards and the Golden Globe Awards, or at least have good word-of-mouth, according to critics. However, these two main goals may not be achieved at the same time.

The dream of a film director is, of course, to win an award for Best Director in reputable film competitions, while the primary goal of a film production company is to make a big profit. There are cases where film production companies invest hundreds of millions of dollars in the movies but eventually incur huge losses. In contrast, the films win some awards or are highly recommended by critics.

Therefore, the goal of film production is crucial and must be clear. Do you want a profitable film or an award-winning film? A famous film director has produced all his movies under budget and has brought significant profits to his producers. However, he has never won an award in any contests.

Adding Goals

When setting the goal, we may have a collection of goals with common results instead of a single goal or goals that achieve the same final result. Once a goal is set, we may have subsets under it. Each subset may have its subsets, and so on. That is, we can keep adding goals to a problem and then select one from them to achieve it or achieve the final goal by achieving each goal in the subsets.

If the problem of a corporation is a decrease in profit, then its goal should be *to increase its profitability*. However, there are several ways to achieve this goal. For example, they can reduce costs (through zero-based budgeting[104] or simplifying company structure), increase sales revenue (by expanding the product line or improving the existing products), or increase the profit margin (by raising prices or boosting productivity).

As a result, the subsets that you are going to create should include "zero-based budgeting", "simplifying company structure", "expanding the product line", "improving the existing products", "increasing the price", "boosting the productivity", etc. This is, in fact, the second level in the goal-setting task. The top-level goal is to increase its profit; the second-level goals are those projects. In bullet points, we have:

➢ Increase the profit level

- zero-based budgeting

- simplifying company structure

- expanding the product line

- improving the existing products

---

104 "Zero-based budgeting", Wikipedia, last accessed August 28, 2020, https://en.wikipedia.org/wiki/Zero-based_budgeting

- increasing the price

- boosting productivity

- ...

To each subset, we may add its own subsets. Take the detergent company as an example. If it wants to increase its profitability, it will have similar bullet points to the above ones. Take *expanding the product line* as an example; we may have *different types of detergents, other cleaning products, cleaning-related products, non-related products, etc.*

If we present the structure in bullet points, it will look like this:

➢ Increase the profit level

- zero-based budgeting

- simplifying company structure

- expanding the product line

  o different types of detergents

  o other cleaning products

  o cleaning related products

  o non-related products

  o ...

- improving the existing products

- increasing the price

- boosting the productivity

- ...

When we convert the bullet points into a tree diagram, it will be easier to trace back the routes, like playing the Ghost Leg[105] game, so that we can identify the details of the steps involved in solving a particular problem. We will talk about this in the next chapter.

Setting a Flow Chart

We have talked about the importance of a flow chart to show every step from the starting point (present state) to the finish line (the goal). When drafting the flow chart, we should move forward and backward to make sure every possible route is included. That is a crucial step as we will use the flow chart to determine all possible solutions to the problem.

Let us take an example: Pretend that you are a high school student and want to be a Cambridge University student. The average high school grade average of students accepted by Cambridge is 95%. The traditional way of thinking is typical, "I have to get a grade average higher than 95% in order to be accepted by Cambridge University". The problem, accordingly, will be: How do I get a grade average higher than 95%?

If you rely on this one-route flow chart to analyze your possibility of being accepted by Cambridge University and your high school grade average is lower than 90%, then you may think that the chance of getting accepted is slim. You may also feel that the only solution to this problem is trying your best to get a higher grade average.

---

[105] "Ghost Leg", Wikipedia, last accessed August 28, 2020, https://en.wikipedia.org/wiki/Ghost_Leg

However, the fact of the matter is that in addition to the high school grade average, there are other qualifications recognized by Cambridge, including using International Baccalaureate[106] scores, enrolling in the Cambridge Pre-U[107] program, and using A-level[108] exam scores. Actually, there are around 20 different qualifications that can be used to fulfill Cambridge's entrance requirements. All of them are listed on the institution's official website. A detailed flow chart should include all these routes.

However, there are at least two alternatives not listed on the Cambridge site. You may apply to the less competitive programs at Cambridge University and transfer to another major (concentration) later. Since many people typically focus on the institution name instead of the degree, you can even stay in the same program without transferring to receive the brand name boost and be placed in an advantageous position when job searching. For example, there were 251 applications to the Department of Philosophy in 2019, but only 51 applicants were given offers. On the other hand, there were 124 applications to the Department of Theology, Religion and Philosophy of Religion, and 58 applicants got offers. That is, an application for the Department of Theology, Religion and Philosophy of Religion has more than two times greater opportunity acceptance than the same application for the Department of Philosophy.

You may also apply for other first-tier universities in the UK, such as the London School of

---

[106] "International Baccalaureate", Wikipedia, last accessed August 28, 2020, https://en.wikipedia.org/wiki/International_Baccalaureate

[107] "Cambridge Pre-U", Wikipedia, last accessed August 28, 2020, https://en.wikipedia.org/wiki/Cambridge_Pre-U

[108] "GCE Advanced Level", Wikipedia, last accessed August 28, 2020, https://en.wikipedia.org/wiki/GCE_Advanced_Level

Economics and Political Science[109] (LSE) and the University College London[110] (UCL), and then apply for a transfer after finishing the first semester or year. I know a gentleman who was not accepted by Cambridge but UCL to study Computer Science. He applied to Cambridge after finishing year one at UCL and was accepted as a freshman in Cambridge. He fulfilled his dream at the cost of repeating the first year in Cambridge, but it was fun, according to him.

---

[109] "London School of Economics", Wikipedia, last accessed August 28, 2020, https://en.wikipedia.org/wiki/London_School_of_Economics
[110] "University College London", Wikipedia, last accessed August 28, 2020, https://en.wikipedia.org/wiki/University_College_London

Chapter 9: Reverse Thinking

Solving a problem is like trying to exit a maze with traps at each turning point, with the *problem* being the *exit* and each *trap* being a *challenge*. Even if you can overcome all the challenges, it does not mean that you can exit the maze because you may be going the wrong way. Different thinking modes can help you break down or avoid the traps but cannot help you determine with absolute certainty the route which will lead you outside the maze. A maze can produce many different routes, short and long, by repeating some of the paths. You must select the shortest route to the exit.

Similarly, there may be several ways to achieve a goal, but the path that you choose may not be a feasible, successful, or effective one. The question we have to ask is: Which way is the one that can achieve the goal most efficiently and effectively?

Ghost Leg is a matching game that consists of a diagram of routes that have the same number of starting points and ending points. Each starting point is linked to a corresponding ending point, and two starting points will never have the same corresponding ending point, nor will an ending point ever lack a corresponding starting point to link to it. If one of the ending points is your target, then there is only one starting point that will lead to your target.

The rule of this game is to choose a starting point and follow its line downwards (or upwards, depending on the drawing). When the vertical line encounters a horizontal line, you must follow it to the next vertical line and then continue moving downwards. Repeat this procedure until you reach the end of a vertical line. You then arrive at an ending point with something associated with it that can be a prize or a task to be completed.

Below is an illustration of a Ghost Leg game with ten starting points, A to J, and ten ending points, 1 to 10.

Starting Points

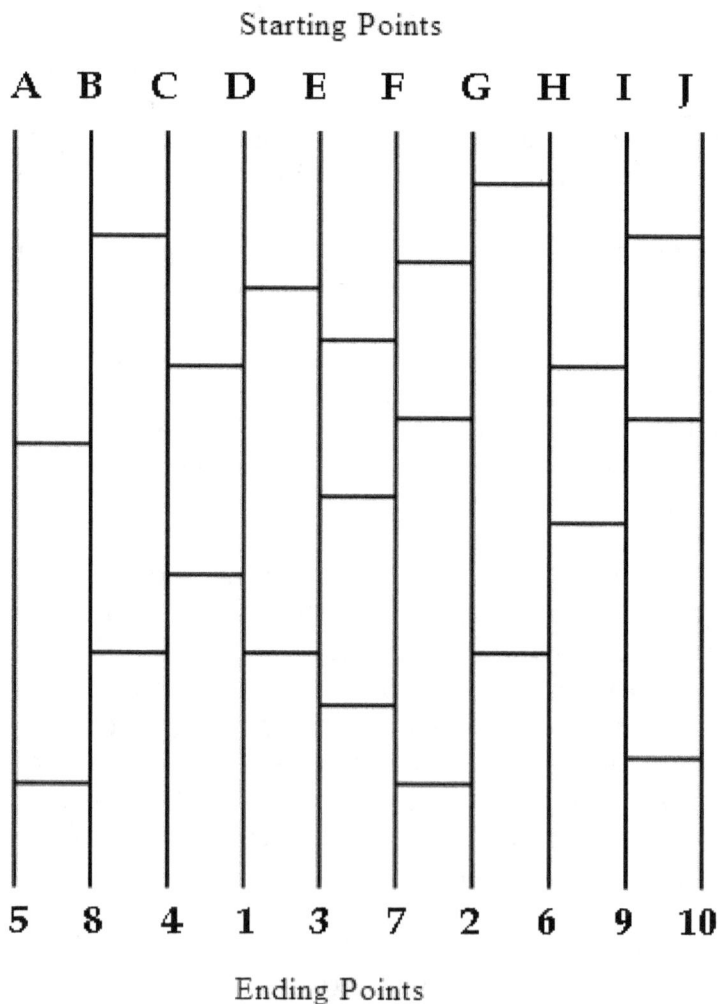

Ending Points

Figure 1

Let us depict an example using Figure 1. Ten people go to a cottage for a week, and there are ten different tasks to be performed by them. To be fair, the ten tasks will be assigned by playing a Ghost Leg game.

All the tasks are represented by the numbers 1 to 10. For instance, let us say that task #1 is to take out the garbage to the dumpsite, while task #10 is to buy food for barbeques. The first person decides to start and chooses 'F' as the starting point. As shown in Figure 2 with the highlighted line, the route will extend from "F" and ultimately end at destination "1". Depending on the starting point, the other nine individuals will consequently end up at other destinations, therefore obtaining different tasks.

At first glance, this may appear to be an arbitrary game in which luck plays an important role. However, once you know the trick of this game, you can always arrive at the destination you want without fail.

The nature of this game is that every starting point will lead to a unique ending point. As such, the trick is to work backwards. By doing so, you can easily predict the result.

Starting Points

A B C D E F G H I J

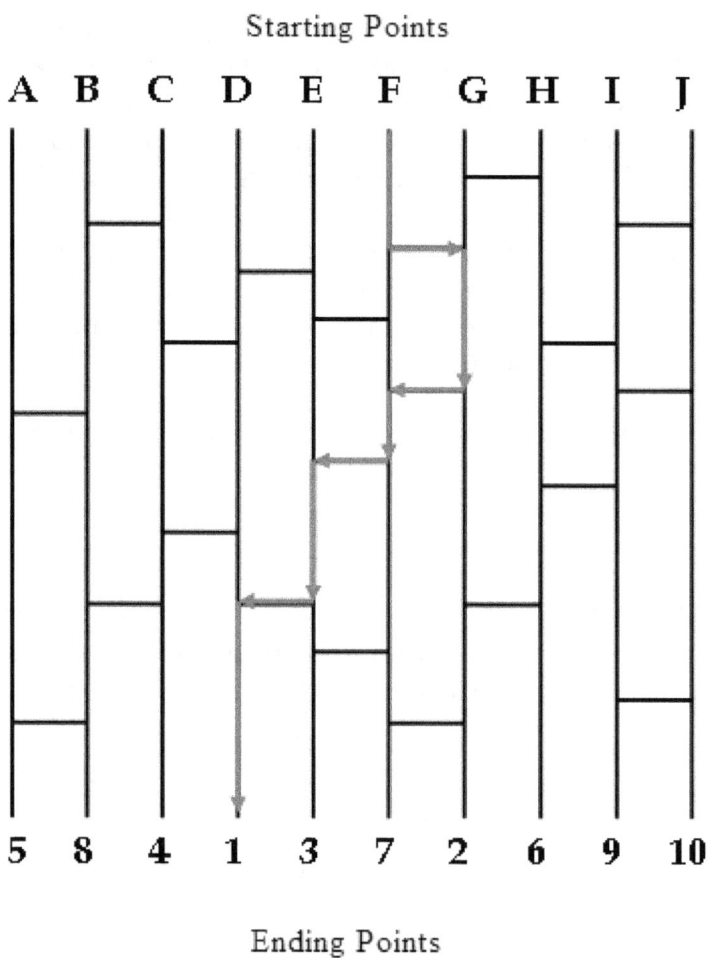

5 8 4 1 3 7 2 6 9 10

Ending Points

Figure 2

Let us assume that you love taking out the garbage to the dumpsite and hate buying food for

96

barbeques. Let us also assume that you are impartial to all the other eight tasks. As such, you want to get to "1" as your destination but want to avoid "10" at all costs.

With this goal in mind, you must choose the correct starting point that will place you in the ideal position. To do so, you should start the game at "1" and work backwards, following the same playing instructions as described before but moving up instead of moving down. In other words, you should choose an ending point that you want to get to and then move back to the starting point. When the vertical line encounters a horizontal line, you must follow it to the next vertical line and then continue upwards.

For instance, when the vertical line extending from ending point "1" encounters a horizontal line, you must follow it and travel to the connecting vertical line. Continue doing so as you move upwards. Eventually, you will end up at "F" (Figure 3).

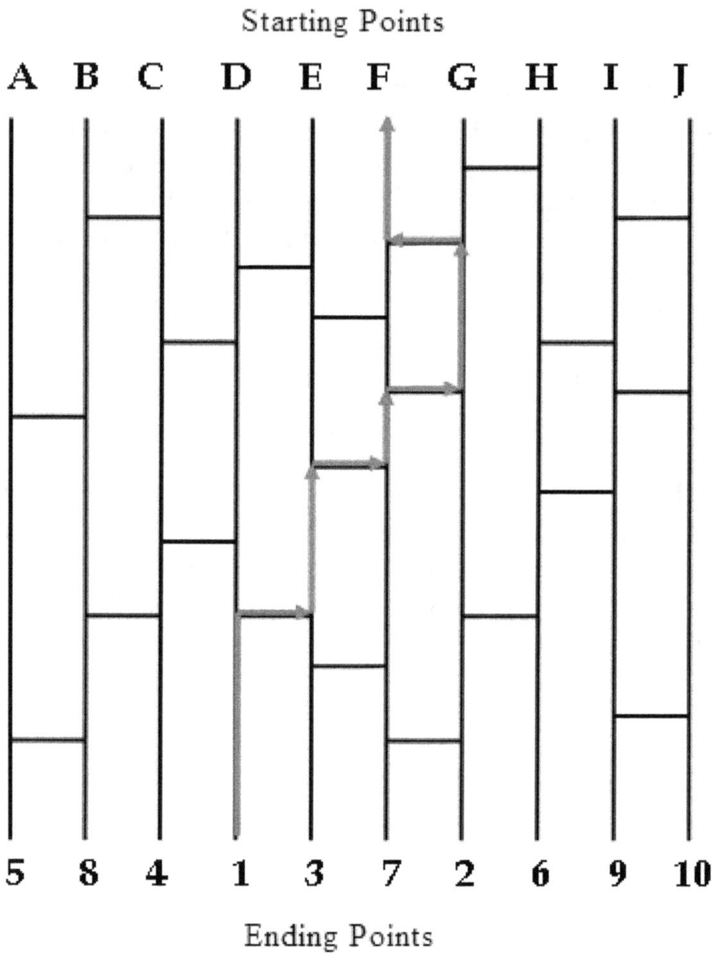

Starting Points

A B C D E F G H I J

5 8 4 1 3 7 2 6 9 10

Ending Points

Figure 3

You can, therefore, pick your preferred outcome
in advance by using this backward trick in a very short

time as compared with trial and error with each route at the starting points. For example, if you want to have task #3, you will know to work backwards, starting from "3" and moving upwards. Consequently, you will know to pick "H" as the starting point.

If, on the other hand, your only goal is to not end up with task #10 (you are impartial to all other nine tasks), you will know to avoid picking "J" as the starting point. You can try this on your own, using the method I have just taught you of working backwards.

If you choose the wrong starting point, you will never be able to arrive at your desired ending point (achieve your goal). This kind of reverse method applies not only to this one-to-one mapping situation but also to all others: one-to-many mapping, many-to-one mapping, and many-to-many mapping.

Let us consider another scenario. There are ten different Ghost Leg games for you to play. Each of them consists of 10 starting points, A to J, and ten ending points, 1 to 10 (a variant of Figure 1, by adding or removing some horizontal lines to it). If you can get to #1 at the ending point in the next game again, you can move on to the next round. That is, you must get #1 to advance in the games. If you can get #1 in all ten games, you will be awarded one million dollars as the prize.

The question is: What is the probability that you can get #1 in all games if you randomly pick the starting point in each game?

Since there is only one out of ten starting points that will bring you to ending point #1, it means that you have a probability of 1/10 to win each game. There are ten games you must win in order to receive the prize, and because each game has a winning probability of

1/10, the probability of winning all ten games is, therefore:

$$1/10 \times 1/10 \times 1/10 \times 1/10 \times 1/10$$

$$\times 1/10 \times 1/10 \times 1/10 \times 1/10 \times 1/10$$

$$= 1/10,000,000,000$$

In other words, if there are 10 billion people who play this game randomly, on average, only one person can get the prize, and the remaining people will fail. This probability is much lower than the odds of winning any lottery ticket in the world. The probability of winning a Powerball jackpot[111] is 1/292,201,338; the probability of winning a Mega Millions jackpot[112] is 1/302,575,350; the probability of winning a Lotto Max jackpot is 1/33,294,800. The odds of winning these jackpots are 30 times higher than the probability of this scenario.

Using the one-to-one mapping characteristic of Ghost Leg, you can apply the reverse method to pick your starting point in each game so that you can guarantee with 100% certainty that you will arrive at destination #1 at the end. That is the basic concept of *reverse thinking* – we start from the final goal to identify the paths and starting points that can lead to the desired outcome.

In real life, people who play Ghost Leg should know this backward trick. Even if they do not know it, they will still cover the middle part of the diagram so that no one can tell how the routes go by using the

---

[111] "Powerball", Wikipedia, last accessed August 28, 2020, https://en.wikipedia.org/wiki/Powerball

[112] "Mega Millions", Wikipedia, last accessed August 28, 2020, https://en.wikipedia.org/wiki/Mega_Millions

trick. These Ghost Leg examples are just used illustratively to show a simplified version of *reverse thinking* and how it can be used to help you solve a problem.

To apply the reverse thinking mode, we need to draw a flow chart illustrating the paths required to reach our goal or a value chain of the whole sequence of events. We must include all the possibilities (routes) that can achieve the goal and move backward from the goal to the starting point to identify the possible solutions or decision points.

Tariffs

A recent example of using a simple reverse thinking technique is regarding the trade war between the United States and China. As the US government imposed a 25% tariff on steel exported from China in 2018, the problem Chinese steel manufacturers were facing was: "*How do we sell steel to the US at a lower cost?*" or "*How can we avoid the tariff?*"

In accordance with the reverse thinking principles, we need to draw a flow chart of the steel trade, beginning from making the steel using iron ore in China to arriving at the warehouse of the US buyers. When we move backwards from the final destination in the US, we will find that when the US Customs inspects imported steel, the 25% tariff will only apply to those exported from China. It means that if we can change the origin of steel, we can lower or even eliminate the 25% tariff. In fact, that was what some Chinese steel manufacturers did after the 25% tariff came into effect.

Most of them moved their production lines to
Vietnam.[113]

A similar situation happened around 20 years ago
to my client, who was the owner of a chain of optical
stores in Canada. He complained about the high tariffs
on eyeglasses frames. After laying out the value chain
and flow of logistics of his products, I added some
alternative routes on the chart to include shipping the
unfinished frames to Canada for assembly. The
"assembly" was simple, just screw the temples (arms)
to the front piece, which was effectively the same
current workload for when the optometrist has to adjust
the frame for the customer. These unassembled frames
were qualified for a lower tariff. As a result, it saved
the client 15% of tariffs.

Writing Machine

I have participated in creating various types of
exams for high school students, college students and
licensed courses. Some of the exams are essay-type
questions, and some of them are multiple-choice
questions.

In some of the multiple-choice exams, the
requirements were that the answers must be in the
textbooks or official learning materials so that the
students would identify the correct answer by referring
to the books or materials. That is, a justification for
each answer was needed, and this justification must
come from the textbooks or official learning materials.
This is quite difficult for non-scientific subjects.

---

[113] "US slaps import duties of more than 400% on Vietnam steel", Wikipedia, last updated
July 3, 2019, https://economictimes.indiatimes.com/news/international/business/us-
slaps-import-duties-of-more-than-400-on-vietnam-steel/articleshow/70063777.cms

In one of the organizations, some of my colleagues found that drafting such exam questions was very challenging, and they were, therefore, relatively slow in writing these prompts. A couple of colleagues could only create two to three questions per day. The learning materials were quite complicated; each key learning point may involve a few pages in different chapters. As each question had to test one particular key learning point, my colleagues had to read all the materials regarding that key learning point and then decide what to ask and how to write the question, which could be quite a time-consuming process.

On the contrary, I could produce fifteen to twenty questions per day and wrote over one thousand questions, earning the title of "writing machine" within my teams. Among all my colleagues, only one of them asked me how I could write that fast. I told him the secret – work using a reverse method.

In a multiple-choice question, it is very difficult to test more than one key learning point unless we make it very complicated. Therefore, the easiest way to draft a question is to work backwards: first, identify the text regarding the key learning point we desire to test (pinpoint the answer first) and then ask the question accordingly. That is also a simple form of *Reverse Thinking*.

Conclusion

The three main steps in problem-solving are Goal Setting, Reverse Thinking and Creative Thinking. How to apply these steps can be explained in the following Q&A.

Q: Why do we need goal-setting?

A: It is because we want to have an achievable goal that can solve our real problem and with more options.

Q: Why do we need reverse thinking?

A: It is because we can find out all the possible paths to achieve the goal, hence being able to pick the easiest or the shortest route. Moreover, when one way is blocked, we have the alternatives ready.

Q: Why do we need creative thinking?

A: It is because when we want to achieve a goal, there are difficulties that the existing methods cannot overcome, so we need new ideas.

Q: How can we think creatively?

A: Repeatedly apply the seven techniques in Chapters 1 to 7.

Whenever we have a problem, we have to set the goal first. When we set a goal, we have to ask ourselves a question: "Why?"

"Why do I want to do it?" or "Why do I need it?" or "Why does it bother me?" etc.

For example, when you are looking for a new job, finding a new job is not your real problem, and finding a new job is not your real goal. You have to ask, *"Why do I want to have a new job?"* The answer may be: "I need more money", or "I don't like my boss," or "I don't like my job responsibilities," or "I need more time to spend with my family", etc.

A different answer will affect the possible solutions to solve your problem. If you want more money, having a part-time job may be a solution; investing your money can also earn more money. Therefore, finding a new job is not the only solution. If you do not like your boss or job responsibility, an internal transfer is also an option. Therefore, it is important to know WHY you want a new job before you take action.

After knowing your goal, we have to draw a flow chart for reaching your goal, with all possible paths back to your current position. If you are a high school student and your goal is to become a Certified Public Accountant (CPA), then you have to know all the possible routes that can become a CPA, including academic and experience requirements. Once you have drawn the flow chart, you can tell which route is the fastest, which one may be the easiest, or which one costs you the least.

On the flow chart that you draw, there may be different stages that you have to achieve. In order to achieve a stage, there will be some difficulties to be overcome. This is the time you have to apply the seven

106

creative thinking techniques to find out the solutions. Keep in mind those techniques can be used alone, together and repeatedly.

By following the three steps of Differential Cogitation – goal setting, reverse thinking and creative thinking, most of the problems can be solved in principle and more effectively and efficiently than by using other methods of thinking.

~ The End ~

www.ingramcontent.com/pod-product-compliance
Lightning Source LLC
LaVergne TN
LVHW051748080426
835511LV00018B/3264